Knowing touch

Published by: IngramSpark Australia (2020)

Peter Levy is predominantly a songwriter with a passion for all sorts of writing.

Of his 17 movie soundtracks, hhis favorite is:

Tread lightly on our land
Directed by: Jon Noble
Film Company: FilmWest (1972)

Other novels by Peter Levy:

System error: the diary of my reconfiguration
Amazon (2018)
Also available on Kindle.
The Book Depository

Betsy Collins
Amazon (2019)
The Book Depository

Latest musical album:
"Don't come back"
https://open.spotify.com/album/3CiWXa1i8ktDXiUw5mOxpt

Author's Note

I would especially like to acknowledge and thank Sharon Hurst for her efforts. Not only for her most excellent contribution on the editing and layout of this novel, but for her tireless support throughout the process. It could not have been completed without her.

I would also like to show my gratitude to the office of IngramSpark Australia. Helpful to the enth degree and always available to chat through every crisis, no matter how small or trivial.

Thanks also to Alex Nutman (a.e.nutman@gmail.com) for preparing the files for upload.

Knowing touch

Peter Levy

Reuben Cohn worked at The Cook County Morgue. He detested the pervading odour of the place so much that his office door was usually shut in an effort to filter out the smell. People opened his door from time to time and on each of these occasions he would keep his head down in a futile attempt to avoid the obnoxiousness. Staff often took his actions as a rejection of all humans, and there was an element of that in Reuben's general mannerisms to support such a theory. Reuben was complex. There was no kinder way to describe him.

The door opened.

"I need whatever you can get from this," said a forensic doctor in a white suit. He handed Reuben a shiny cylinder. In it was a newly-removed brain.

Cradling the cylinder, Reuben immediately crossed to a large refrigerated cabinet that hummed softly, and was run by a powerful motor. The contents needed to be kept as fresh as possible, as they were inviariably various body parts, mostly human, but sometimes of an unknown origin.

As he waited, the doctor gazed around the office trying to imagine what it was that Reuben actually did with the specimens that came his way. He was obviously well respected among his colleagues, but this office was so small compared to the doctor's laboratory that he couldn't see what everyone was raving about. This guy Reuben was not even a doctor.

"Looking for anything in particular?" Reuben asked almost casually without making any eye contact.

"Murder case, man. He might know who did it to him. We sure don't."

"What happened to the rest of him?"

"Acid. Lucky to get the brain intact."

"Ok, I'll get to it after I finish with this one I'm working on," said Reuben, quite detached from the grisly scenario he had just heard described.

The forensics doctor left the office quite bemused and confident that Reuben, with all his apparent arrogance, would not achieve anything more than what his team had.

Reuben Cohn was twenty-five going on fifty, gangly and tall for his age with jet black hair and brown eyes that never seemed to show any emotion at all. Perfect for working with pieces of brains and body parts that resembled no-one in particular. He had been studying to become a doctor when he answered an advertisement that effectively scotched his studies. By joining the DA's office in downtown Chicago he now had an opportunity to leave home and to earn some real money. The advert simply said they were looking for people with specific qualities who had completed at least first year of medical school.

At the interview, when the deal was fully presented to him, it was clear that he was the right loner for the job. Long hours on great wages with benefits that required the winning applicant to work by themselves, after initial training, and extract as much knowledge as possible to assist in building profiles of what they assessed might have happened to the victims – mostly victims of some crime, accident cases, insurance claims against hospitals, birth defects and drowning.

The Cook County Morgue had several offices set aside for the DA's department and was located in the seedier part of town at 2121 West Harrison Street. Rent was cheap and not too many middle-class people ever went near it. You would have to be looking for the place to find it, nestled amongst apartment blocks and elementary schools. It was not an area to visit. Especially at night. Stumbling into it usually meant you were lost and had taken a wrong turn in some vain attempt to beat the city traffic on your way home. It was not a place to park your car either, as the crime rate here was significantly higher than in other areas of the city.

Members of the general Chicago population who met with an unexpected demise had either their cadavers, or parts thereof, sent to this morgue for identification purposes before being claimed and buried. Criminals and victims of crime usually also ended up here for forensic studies.

Reuben had been on the job for the past five years with rarely a day off. He was the kind of nerd who didn't have any friends to speak of and had moved away from the warmth of his family, such as it was, when he decided to drop out of med school. With his middle-class Jewish background, this was one thing that you just didn't do. No family and no real friends meant he lived alone. The single room flat opposite the morgue suited him wonderfully. Work and home became one and the same for Reuben. It didn't seem to matter to him at all.

For years scientists had been mystified by memory functions within the brain. But recently, a new technology was being tested by The Cook County Morgue. The cutting edge machinery could preserve human tissue, as well as isolate memory neurons to gain valuable insights and reenactments.

Purpose-created for this was the BT100, a very new and different machine which needed to be firstly connected to a computer and calibrated. This was state of the art technology that very few people in the world even knew existed. Invented some four years earlier by The Baring Medical Research Company out of Toronto, the Chicago morgue was the guinea pig to see if there would be any real value from the information gleaned from it.

Of all possible body parts that made their way into his domain, Reuben loved to work on brains. He was the first one to realize the BT100's full potential and relished his time on it. He even made plenty of minor adjustments, both on the software that ran it and the hardware that housed it, to suit particular situations and that made the BT100 a totally different beast from the one sent down by TBMRC. Their technicians would, on occasion, drop by to service the machine and try a few things out as experiments. The machine was now Reuben's as the manual no longer had relevance thanks to Reuben's adjustments. The technicians stopped coming and Reuben serviced the machine himself. It was his and his alone. If a perfect scenario for him existed then this was definitely it. No-one else understood what he did and not too many people had the patience to listen to his in-depth monotonous monologues on the subject. No-one would ever go back for second chat with Reuben. Results, ultimately, were the key elements in the department and Reuben delivered them every time.

The main reason Reuben's employers had selected him to work on this ground-breaking project, was their early observations of his abnormally focussesd and obsessional nature. No-one in the department could come close to his knowledge and grasp of what it took to get relevant information from machines and then to interepret it in a way that made sense to forensic investigators. They all left him to work alone and in some respects took him for granted. Most employees who worked there had in fact never even met him. Reuben preferred it like that too.

Turning his attention back to his current case, Reuben unplugged the four electrodes which connected a severed arm to the KL33. This was a clever little machine, small enough to sit on his desk, and capable of determining basic information about any body part attached to it. In this case, the specimen was from a victim of a crime that had very few clues for the investigators to go on. Reuben scrutinized the electronic readout from the machine, and methodically began to compile his report on what he found, rapidly tapping the keys of his computer.

Knife wound from a kitchen bread knife caused the initial entry point and severing arteries S7 and S8. Fresh bread crumbs indicated the time of day to be roughly seven thirty in the morning. Type of bread was "Light Rye". Two other wounds on the arm were made from a different knife. Possibly a pocket knife with a four inch blade. I suggest a Swiss Army Knife, model number A234-32. Assailant was left-handed, judging from the angles of the cuts. Victim's arm had been in river water for at least two days. Blood type is B.

Reuben was in no hurry as he plastic-bagged the arm and placed it in the dispatch section of the refrigerated filing cabinet. He knew that rushing on any part of the procedural process would invariably open the door for elements to be missed. Being a perfectionist, there was no way he would do that. His initial training on the job had been clear and precise, and his methodology was nothing less than rigorous. Even though he never, as a rule, followed up on any case after he had handed it back, he knew instinctively that his work was vital in the forensic presentation of a case. It was the fine details that could eliminate or incriminate a suspect. Reuben simply didn't concern himself with who, where and why. That was other people's work and he rarely interfered or was interested in it. He gave each job his total attention, but when his final report was made he never thought about it again.

When Reuben first secured his position with the morgue, there were a few people who would say quite nasty and hurtful things to him, just to see the effect it would have. Their amusement soon came to the attention of the senior management and an inter-office memo circulated.

Reuben Cohn is no longer to be the bunny for your jokes. He is too important and we will not tolerate any further taunting of him. Instant dismissal is the consequence.

One case worker, who openly laughed at the memo as not enforceable, was subsequently let go and everyone knew that Reuben was off-limits and not to be communicated with unless strictly for morgue business. Reuben was left alone and this suited him to the point that he felt secure and happy for the first time in his miserable life.

Reuben disposed of the latex gloves he was using for the arm and put on a fresh pair. Without any emotion he carefully unpacked the brain from its cylindrical container and started to place electrodes into twenty-two specific positions. From previous procedures he had ascertained these to be the most beneficial. One by one he connected leads to the electrodes and plugged them into the BT100. Before turning the machine on, he made sure the connection to his personal computer was secure and that the computer was active and primed to receive the BT100 by going into the program specifically designed for it. All looked normal. Reuben turned the machine on and waited for the brain to be 'talking' to the BT100 and then set the computer to record as much of it as he could.

Very carefully Reuben isolated the first of the twenty-two electrodes and tapped the record button. Data started to flow. This first electrode was for audio sounds that the brain may have made or received during the final days or weeks when alive and functioning in a body. Sometimes the information had erased itself when the body and brain ceased to live. There was no way to know what was available or usable without going through the process. Reuben knew from experience that he would have to watch that screen for the next twenty-three hours to make sure there were no stoppages.

Reuben's mobile phone buzzed in his pocket and he glanced at it. Seeing it was his mother he answered it with a level of trepidation.

"Hello."

"Reuben, it's your mother."

"I know."

"How are you?"

"Well. What do you want?"

"Inviting you for dinner on Friday."

"What day is it now?"

"Tuesday."

"Not sure. Very busy right now."

"Alright, see if you can fit it into your busy schedule then," she said sarcastically.

"Ok. Goodbye."

"Nice to chat with you Reuben. We love you."

Reuben heard the last words of love and pushed the end call button on his mobile to resume his vigil. The screen kept emitting random garbage but Reuben found it fascinating and every so often he would write a note regarding a place on the file to go back to that looked interesting.

The hours passed. Meals and sleep were overlooked as the screen dominated Reuben's mind. Somewhere he was trying to make some analytical sense of the data flow but was not quite able to secure a formula for the patterns that he was observing. It didn't matter that much to Reuben but did give him something to consider and focus on.

It was exactly twenty-three hours, forty-four minutes and seventeen seconds when the brain ceased to emit anything new. Deciding he needed a stroll, Reuben unplugged the electrode from the BT100, packed the brain back into its cylinder and placed it in the refrigerated cabinet. All part of his thorough and practised procedure.

Reuben walked out of the morgue through a side exit to which he had the combination security code and marched across the road to his apartment block. The wind had picked up quite a bit and Reuben shielded his eyes from the dust and swirling leaves. He was used to the vagaries of the wind, having lived in Chicago all his life. They didn't call it "The Windy City" for nothing.

A few of the more elderly regular tenants nodded to Reuben as he approached the building. He attempted an acknowledgement by readjusting his baseball hat as if it was a ritual salute. They never attempted an actual conversation with Reuben. It was a case of mutual tolerance. They felt he was a little weird, as well as being ultra-quiet, but he hadn't done anything bad to them. There was never a case where he was the subject of a complaint, like many others were. Reuben simply had no wish to converse with anyone. He had been there for almost five years and was known as a loner and that his privacy was his own business and should be respected. Five years in that apartment block was quite a long time compared to the large proportion of other renters who were very transient. Reuben was hardly there anyway. He basically just used the place to eat, sleep and shower. The morgue was his real home. Deep down, Reuben often considered his neighbours as future specimens that he might have to work on one day so he didn't really want any attachments that might pop up in his laboratory.

Reuben's apartment was ultra basic. A bed, a kitchen table with two chairs that seemed a bit out of place or just hopeful. No-one ever visited. An IBM computer that was connected to a big screen television, a mid-sized fridge, smallish stove and a microwave oven. His cupboard was filled with cans of baked beans, spaghetti, salads and sardines, very skillfully stacked in precise rows of three, with the writing facing forward. Everything was neat and orderly, providing a certainty that made him feel secure.

The external windows were always shaded to keep the eyes of the world out. He was used to living like an underground mole. It was not that he hated people, but more of a self-realisation that his coping skills were not well developed. A balance was maintained and generally worked well. Reuben was a creature of balance and could not quite understand the inconsistencies he often encountered in his interactions with other humans.

His school days had been a nightmare. No contact with anyone. Upon finishing school each day, the taunting ceased and solitude became his comfort of choice. Study was pleasurable. Unlike many fellow students, Reuben wrote copious amounts of facts and figures down in several exercise books and would memorize each page. In this way, over time, he developed unique skills that helped him to survive; skills that were a substitute for the lack of friends and his total social ineptitude.

A nice long hot shower was what he wanted and the steam permeated throughout the apartment. More paint slowly stripped from the walls. Cheap paint. Very little air ventilation existed as the solitary ceiling fan in his bathroom had long since clogged up and ceased to operate. Reuben always turned the switch on but of late nothing ever happened with it. He didn't notice. It was simply a routine that held no significance and, as it turned out, absolutely no functionality.

After drying himself off, Reuben opened a can of sardines and hungrily devoured it. Sleep was next on his agenda and he collapsed onto his bed and let eight hours roll by in what seemed like the blink of his closing eyelid.

The actual time of day and the day of the week were also totally irrelevant to Reuben and, luckily for him, not so important to the bosses of the morgue either. They themselves were prone to be workaholics too, when the occasion warranted. It was not unusual to see people coming and going at any hour of the day or night. The main entrance was manned by two security guards at all times on permanent eight-hour shifts. Public holidays included. Even Christmas.

Around two o'clock in the morning, in total darkness, Reuben left his apartment. Intermittent loud music came from an upstairs unit but the only living thing Reuben encountered was a stray tabby cat that, oddly enough, was known to him. He had on occasion fed it the leftover of some canned fish when the cat sometimes came calling.

"Not tonight puss. Got to work" Reuben spoke in a tender tone to the cat and stroked its neck. The cat purred expectantly.

Feeling the soft fur of the tabby. Reueben suddenly was aware of an image that flashed through his brain. It wasn't completely clear, but he could make out two alley cats copulating and yowling. Reuben put it down to his own tiredness and vivid imagination. The sensation was over as quickly as it had appeared.

Shielding his eyes from the still-swirling breeze of nine hours earlier, Reuben crossed the near empty road, and made his way back into the morgue. All the lights were on, as was the standard practice, so it was easy for him to find the right corridor and re-enter his domain again.

He was very eager to get back to his office so that he could analyze the audio that he was certain had been emitted by the brain he was in the middle of examining.

Once esconced in his chair, he switched on his computer drive. Countless numbers, incomprehensible to the average person's eye, started flowing across the screen. As it flicked past him, Reuben's concentration was unwavering. Occasionally he would re-wind a section and, once fully convinced that it held nothing of any significance, would delete it from the hard drive. There were twelve terabytes of data to work with and the computer groaned and slowed at every opportunity. Having less data to work with had to be better, he reasoned. Not deleting valuable information was Reuben's unique specialty. He was fastidious and diligent not to ever shortcut any of his procedural routines.

Mostly, the data was composed of dots and dashes, zeros and ones. What he was searching for was anything that resembled a wave file hidden amongst it. Whenever such a file appeared, Reuben would isolate it, copy it to another drive and examine it. To do this he employed an audio program that was linked to two hi-fidelity studio speakers that would pick up on anything remotely resembling human speech or any other possibly significant noise. A pair of powerful Sennheiser HD 820 headphones were also plugged into the hi-fi. Reuben often put them on to listen more intently to the noise coming from the computer. There was no way of knowing what was about to be heard and sometimes it was so soft in tone that a boost from the headphones was very necessary.

Four such episodes resulted in garbled nonsense that gave Reuben some heart that more was around that could and would be useful. The garbled files he put into a special folder as he figured that, even though he couldn't make any sense out of it, someone else might. If not now, then in years to come when the technology improved. Technology was always bettering itself. There were constant updates to the audio software and Reuben always bought them to be fully state of the art. It was his business and he couldn't afford not to be at the cutting edge. Anyway, the morgue paid for everything, including the food he ate while he was working there. The DA's department thought of everything to keep him content and working effectively. He soldiered on, ordered breakfast from the canteen and didn't even look up to acknowledge its delivery when it was placed on a table near to his desk. No-one dared disturb Reuben while he was working. He was off-limits.

Donning the Sennheiser once more, Reuben turned his attention to the fifth audio episode. He turned the volume up to its maximum so that the crackles could be deciphered. Just as he was beginning to think this was another dead end, with nothing but static, something different caught his attention. The waves on the screen began to oscillate violently and what could only be a human voice burst into the headphones.

The words "I warned you!" were followed by an explosive sound that Reuben knew from experience was a gunshot.

From those three words there were definite traceable elements. Reuben played the file again and again, filtered the gunshot to a separate folder and trawled the internet on a hunch. He went straight to the Beretta catalogue and saw the handgun he was searching for. Reuben used his DA clearance to access the library of sounds associated with a multitude of weapons and soon zeroed in on the Beretta 92FSR-22 - Sniper Grey. Very popular with Mossad and

CIA operatives as it had special grooves already in place for a compact silencer to be easily fitted, used and then disassembled. Taking a copy of the sound, Reuben pasted it into the software program, compared it to the sound sequence extracted from the brain, and bingo! There was a series of matches that gave a score of ninety-five percent assurance that this model was the one used on the body that this brain had once been a vital part of.

As excited as he was, Reuben realized it was still early days as far as completing the audio analysis but here was a voice print and a known weapon used. Procedural practice kicked in, and, efficiently creating a new document, he wrote a brief report which he dutifully emailed to his boss, Special Agent Steve Goodall.

Reuben's breakfast was cold by now but that didn't faze him one little bit. Cold coffee and an egg and mayo sandwich were eaten in a flash. He had always been known as a fast and voracious eater. Even from his childhood days, if anything edible was to his liking and placed in front of him, then he saw no reason to delay the process of getting it into his mouth and then swallowing it, much to the constant annoyance of his family, especially his mother who was trying in vain to teach Reuben better table manners.

"Eat slower and chew your food like everyone else does," she would say to him constantly.

"I don't know everyone else," was one of his stock replies.

From his teenage years on, his eating habits were never discussed in front of him again. It was pointless. In his parents' opinion, there were some things he was never going to learn or change and this was going to be one of them.

Special Agent Steve Goodall's name flashed up on his phone and before it had actually rung, Reuben had the cellphone to his ear.

"Boss! You like?"

"You bet Reuben. Keep up the good work. Let me know if anything else turns up, will you?"

"Will do. Goodbye." Reuben hit the disconnect and resumed his wave file search.

This was a long and tedious process. Reuben deleted another three terabytes of data before discovering a further potential file. He downloaded it and placed the Sennheiser over his ears a bit like a musical producer would do in a recording studio. There was something there, but the signal was too weak and the wave file too small to boost any further than he was already doing. It was extremely frustrating.

Reuben had installed a Logic Pro program, five months back, for more in-depth manipulations of waves or MP3s, so he started it up. He had never used it for this purpose before and so expected there to be a lot of trial and error as he learnt to navigate it.

Reuben discovered very quickly that there was no need to learn everything about a program to use it and get the results required. Even studio professionals rarely understood more than forty percent of what this program could achieve. Home users would probably average around six percent and still be enormously happy with the outcomes it gave them. Reuben was a fast learner when it came to focusing in on electronic gizmos. It was the way he was built. He understood and identified more with machines than he did with humans. He thrived on the lack of emotion and humanity.

Starting up a new "event" on Logic Pro was easier than Reuben had expected. He placed the wave file onto one of the grids and could see that there were filters he could use to further boost the volume without interfering too much with the integrity of the original file. A new voice became audible.

"Helen 712958SU419IV."

Reuben played this new and puzzling sequence over a few times before saving it as a .wav file and transferring it to the folder in which he had stored the previous files.

Audio files were curious things. A musical audio file bears a time and date stamp on it if you know where to look. These extracted audio files however had once been part of the memory of a living human brain, so they bore no such stamp. Exactly when these audio memories were captured and stored was an unknown factor. It could be recent or years ago. Simply finding an audio file from brainwave analysis did not necessarily mean a connection to what had befallen this particular victim under investigation. There was no way of gleaning that sort of information. The science was too new to be precise.

Still, it could be another valuable piece of information, a clue. A different voice print, another name to store for future reference that might hold some key as yet unknown.

Then there was the number. The way the numbers were recorded meant nothing to Reuben. From his previous investigations he instantly knew they were not Swiss bank account numbers as he had initially hoped they might be.

Playing a hunch, he ran the letters and numbers combination into Google. Not one suggestion. He then took the letters out of the combination and ran it again. Up came a photo titled "topless male with facial hair". He duly noted it and took a copy of the picture and the site from where it was obtained for his report. The picture in fact came from Shutterstock, a well-known service which provided a few free, and many more paid for, photos to internet users.

Reuben emailed his report with the picture as an attachment to Special Agent Steve Goodall and went back to his vigil.

An email response from Goodall soon bleeped onto Reuben's screen and he smiled at it.

Very good work, Reuben. Keep it up.

It only took a few words from this man to make a world of difference to Reuben. There was no-one else whose words had the impact that this man's had. Special Agent Steve Goodall was his only link to the bigger world that he inhabited and it meant a great deal for Reuben to be seen, by Steve, as a worthy cog in the wheels that turned. A sense that what he was was useful to The Department was so important to Reuben. Probably more so than anything else in his life at the moment. He truly felt he was born for the job and so fortunate he had secured it.

Feeling hungry again, Reuben dialed the canteen and was quite frustrated when the line rang out. Glancing at his watch he saw that it was two-thirty and he wondered if it was AM or PM. A glance at his computer screen validated that it was in fact PM and so he fast-dialed the number again. Same result.

They were supposed to be open until five every day during the week, thought Reuben, and then another thought hit him. Maybe it's the weekend? Probably is. Missed the family dinner again too. Food's nice but the conversation seemed more like an interrogation than anything else. *I'm starving but pretty glad I missed being there, not that I was really planning to go*, he thought.

Reuben locked up his office and headed out of the building back across the street to his apartment block. There was a group of black kids playing basketball on the footpath using a makeshift hoop into which they expertly lobbed balls from quite a distance. They stopped and gazed at Reuben for a few seconds and he noted it in his peripheral vision without looking directly at them.

Reuben picked up his pace so that he was home safe in a very short space of time. He needn't have been worried, as the kids were more concerned with Reuben than he was with them. They noticed the building he came out of and probably suspected he was a cop. Fear is its own master and all loners and losers had it. Reuben knew how to fake bravado but inwardly he was a total mess. He was tired and hungry, as usual, having not slept or eaten properly for the past four days.

Once inside his apartment, Reuben went through a similar routine as he had a few days earlier. A can of sardines on a few dry crackers, a cup of hot tea, steaming shower and then bed. Exhausted, he slept like a baby for twelve hours straight and felt extremely refreshed when he woke. He had been dreaming of the black kids on the road as if they were there to spy on him. As if it had something to do with his work on the brain. It was very confusing and quite strange that he could remember the minutiae of the dream too. Usually he didn't. As he ate a whole can of spaghetti for his breakfast, he puzzled over what it meant and wrote a note into his cellphone that he needed to get more cans of food at the store and that he should eat some fruit and some green vegetables if they were available. Remnants of his mother's instructions.

Outside, the weather had picked up again. A howling wind was using the apartment block as a wind tunnel, whipping up leaves and rubbish of all descriptions from all over the area and dumping it, not so neatly, throughout the grounds. Even for Reuben's standard, which wasn't high, the block looked more disreputable than it had a few days earlier but at heart he didn't really care that much.

As bored as ever, and itching to get back to his audio analysis, Reuben ventured out into the pitch black night, crossed the empty road and let himself into the morgue. This was his entertainment as well; if truth be told, he probably would have done the job he was doing for nothing if the authorities had offered to pay for his accommodation and food. Luckily, this was not the case and most of the money he earned went straight into a bank account that was now looking very healthy. His credit card took care of the odd trips to the stores for food and maybe a new pair of undies when the elastic went.

Reuben had six pairs of undies, all different colors, that he rotated irregularly until they showed signs of normal wear and tear. He would continue to wear them, promising himself to replace them very soon. He only changed them after he showered and that could be a couple of days apart. On one occasion he noticed that his undies had slipped down around his knees, but it still took him until he showered to do anything at all about it. He was good at putting up with things that didn't have a real value to him. The only place where he would never consider shortcutting, or putting up with anything that needed replacing or fixing, was his work environment. The morgue was his dominion that had to be up to date, pristine and clean at all times.

Refreshed, and pleased to be back, Reuben set himself up to continue the hunt. It felt at times a bit like searching for extraterrestrials from a faraway planet, but for Reuben it was sheer pleasure and joy. To scan data and imagine combinations of numbers and symbols meaning something he hadn't quite got a grasp on was exciting. He truly felt that there were clues all around and he was missing them. His challenge was to solve the mysteries and decipher the unknown codes before he could relax and feel totally satisfied with himself. He had a belief that everything would fall into place and be crystal clear sooner or later. In Reuben's case, he wished it to be sooner. Putting more order in the cosmos seemed the only real reason he was put here on this planet. He wanted to know more about things and less about humans. *We are the worst species on the Earth*, he often thought.

Volumes of data passed before his eyes and he deleted most of it. Then there it was: another wave-like file floating in the sea of numbers. Delighted, he isolated it and saved it to his computer. Donning the headphones once again he played it.

"Never forget the number, Simon."

After playing it over and over, Reuben was convinced that the voice signature was the same as the previous one. Using a special spectrogram program, he compared the two files and felt a great sense of satisfaction when the computer gave him a ninety-six percent comparison accuracy. *Was this important? Who was Simon?* he pondered.

Without much further thought, Reuben wrote a report assessing this new piece of possible evidence and emailed it to his boss. Now down to the last terabyte to be checked, Reuben took a break and wandered down the empty halls of the morgue. He poked his nose into two of the storage and autopsy rooms as there was not a soul around. Apart from the guard at the entrance, Reuben was the only living person in the place. Little wonder since it was the wee hours of Sunday morning.

"I suppose I'll end up here too in due course," muttered Reuben to himself.

The self-imposed break came abruptly to an end as guilt over not completing the job swept over him. He knew he was delaying the finishing of the audio as it was the one part of working with brains that he really was keen on and he didn't want it to end just yet. But there were other facets of the investigation that needed his expertise and with that in mind he scurried like a disturbed rabbit back to his warren.

The last terabyte proffered up no new insights into the brain's identity and so it too was deleted. Just under one terabyte was all that Reuben retained for future reference. There was absolutely no more that he could glean from it.

He now tenderly retrieved the brain from its temporary

residence and carefully wired the electrodes back into the BT100 and then into his computer. He was now on the trail for any possible visuals that might still be lurking, in reasonable condition, within the brain. It was a time-consuming long shot.

Over his four years working with this machine, Reuben had worked on eleven brains but only once did one offer up a pixilated image. That too needed to be reconstructed by the experts downtown. The trouble was that digital information was totally inadmissible as evidence in any court. The DA knew that the laws on digital evidence were so precise that any hint of manipulation was a safe bet to have the whole case thrown out of court by any of the young canny lawyers from the new breed of defense attorneys.

This form of evidence was strictly for the DA's office and the investigators to build case profiles. They would then use the evidence with potential witnesses, pretending they knew more than they did, in the hope of getting their hands on "real" evidence.

This was a relatively new science and everyone who knew about its existence had to tread warily and carefully. There were governmental laws that specialized in this form of intellectual property. The big fear was, of course, that individuals or governments could have the tools at their disposal to know more about a person than the person did about themselves. Subconscious thoughts and beliefs may not have yet filtered through to the conscious part of their brains. Perhaps thoughts and feeling were suppressed due to peer group pressures, especially those that dictated acceptable sexual preferences. This was a very fraught area where the traps could be devastating and totally out of left field.

The work that Reuben did and its results were in no way the topic of small talk after work with colleagues in a bar on the East Side. A snooping young reporter once found himself in a bar, listening at great length to a tale from a sacked, resentful and drunk employee, who started to ramble on about some sort of secret work being undertaken at The Cook County Morgue. The reporter was convinced he was onto a scoop, something which could make or break the life of journalists in this town. If they got lucky and managed to impress the editors of the major papers, like *The Tribune*, they were more or less guaranteed a secure income from then on. So the ambitious fellow sniffed around the morgue for a week or two, before being laughed out of the place. Special Agent Steve Goodall managed the situation perfectly by letting him go into every office he wanted to, even Reuben's, and simply exploded with a snort of genuine laughter at every suggestion that they could gain audio and visual information from dead bodies and brains. Goodall was good at deception.

"Science fiction! I sure would love that to be the case. Save me a lot of legwork, I can tell you," Goodall laughed at him.

By the end of the PR process, the reporter was totally convinced it was a dead end and never wasted another neuron chasing the story any further. The disgruntled talkative ex-employee of the morgue was, from that point in time, regarded by nearly all the newspapers in Chicago, as not being a reliable source on any matter relating to The Cook County Morgue and its operations. In fact, the whole episode became the subject of much humour.

Reuben proceeded methodically. He opened the decoding program on his desktop computer and once again sat glued to the flow of data that emanated from the brain. The general binary nature of the zeros and ones soon became a blur and it was only when a different sequence of symbols flashed by that Reuben was jolted back to reality. For the most part, Reuben had the ability to slip into an automated drive state where his eyes and brain would filter the data flow without his conscious self being totally aware of it. A bit like a route you have driven a thousand times before and, on some occasions, not being able to remember any detail about the trip other than the start and end points.

The function of the decoding program was to detect any group of symbols, letters or numbers that could hold visual properties. When a sequence was detected a buzzer would go off so that Reuben could isolate the data, save it into a special folder, then continue the search. He knew, from experience, that most buzzer alerts were false alarms, but he couldn't risk the chance that it might be something of value. It was always a case of Reuben versus the machine. As smart and focused as he was, there was no way he could match his computer in this exercise. Reuben had such a level of respect and admiration for his computer that he would sometimes even chat to it like a friend., not that he had ever had a friend.

A level-ten chess game against the computer had been running for the past two weeks in the background. There was no need to rush into the next move and Reuben used the game as a respite from his work. Whenever the load of watching endless data became too boring or confusing, he would switch it off and go for a stroll. Sometimes, he would go back to his chess game and spend an hour machinating over why the computer had made its last move. He hadn't made a move in over a week. This was not unusual. Moves were unusual. This was not the only chess game Reuben was involved in either.

Four days of wrangling the brain data went by in exactly this manner. Maybe boring for some people. Not for Reuben. As intense as ever, his gaze at the computer screen was continual. He had organized the settings on his PC so that the screen never timed out. Inactivity, or perceived inactivity by the computer, were overridden by the command that the screen stay bright and active. Plenty of buzzing and isolating, but nothing that seemed worthy of being identified as current evidence. Despite mounting frustration, Reuben knew he must persevere.

The long procedure finally ended, and the data flow had found not one usable image. It was time to unwire the brain and pack it away. Reuben wasn't totally ready to do that. He simply sat and stared at the brain for forty minutes before slowly and reluctantly unwiring the electrodes.

Suddenly an outrageous idea started to form in his mind. Remembering his experience with the stray cat from the apartment block, he peeled off his latex gloves, went to the sink and thoroughly washed his hands twice. Returning to his desk, he then placed both hands gently on the exposed brain.

Nothing could have prepared him for the terrifying images that began to flash through his mind: There was absolutely no doubt that he was somehow receiving an image from this disembodied brain. Fear coursed through his every fibre. Fighting the instinct to remove his hands and leave well enough alone, he inexplicably felt driven to take his dramatic methodology to the next level. With shaking hands, one by one, Reuben placed the same twenty-two electrodes onto his own head, approximating where they had been positioned on the brain he had just unwired. He then wired the electrodes into the BT100, made sure the connection to his own computer was secure and then ran the record program.

Reuben knew exactly what he was looking for. He disregarded the recent images that his brain emitted of chess games, the black kids in the school yard and the lustful stray cat. Surprisingly, it didn't take all that long for a clear sequence to emerge. A white male, with no distinguishing features and wearing a dark suit, was holding a gun aimed fair and square towards the head of the victim.

My God! He had it! Here was the killer and the exact moment of the shooting.

Reuben quickly unwired himself and isolated the sequence into a special folder. The face of the man was as clear as crystal. He was no-one that Reuben knew, that was for sure. There was some conversation from the killer but the audio, this time around, could not be salvaged. Reuben went back to the retrieved audio from a few days back, activated his movie-making program, Adobe Premier Pro, and placed it into a fresh file. He then placed the new visual sequence directly above it so that the mouth movements of the killer matched the audio. It was a perfect fit.

"Wow!" said Reuben out loud, "how neat was that!"

Excitedly, Reuben picked up his mobile phone and hit the redial.

"Reuben? Better be important. Do you know what time it is?" said the sleepy, angry voice of Special Agent Steve Goodall.

"It's me. Yes it is important. No, I don't know what time it is."

"OK, what do you have?"

"I've found the face of the killer. But you'll have to come here for me to show it to you and explain it."

"Yeah, I'd say that was important!" grunted Goodall into the phone. "I'll be there in twenty minutes. Great work, Reuben!"

"Thanks Boss," said Reuben with a very pleased look on his face.

Reuben glanced at his watch which read ten past four. It had to be morning by the way Agent Goodall had mentioned the time. What the actual day was, was another question. Reuben had no idea at all. Glancing across at his computer he noticed the time and date. It was Saturday morning.

At twenty to five a very casual looking Goodall, unshaven, beanie on his head, track suit instead of his usual snappy black suit, swaggered through Reuben's door.

"I'm here. What can you tell me?"

"First look at this video, Boss, and I'll explain how I got

it. OK?" asked Reuben seriously.

"Play away. It better be good," muttered Goodall slumping into a chair that faced the computer screen. Reuben had it all set up.

"Oh, it's good alright," said Reuben as he pressed the play button.

The sequence only took 15 seconds but it had Goodall jumping out of his seat.

"I know this guy!" he exclaimed, now fully alert and awake.

Reuben played the sequence again, this time turning up the volume to accentuate the gunshot for maximum effect. He didn't have to do that. He just wanted to.

"This is hot stuff, Reuben. What do you need to tell me? Be brief. I know how in-depth you can be and frankly I don't think I'm up for an hour-long explanation," he blurted out.

Everyone avoided Reuben on discussions, it was well understood, but Goodall was a smart man and his relationship with Reuben was extremely important and he sensed he needed to know what Reuben was about to tell him.

"This video didn't come from the victim's brain, Boss."

"What! You dragged me here ..."

"It came from my brain."

Reuben let the words sink in before continuing to explain what had happened with the alley cat and how he had tried something a bit different to achieve this result.

"You want me to believe you are a psychic now?" Goodall gave him a look that bordered on contempt.

"I'm not sure what I am, but I can tell you that when I touched a stray cat earlier I felt and saw something from that animal. When I touched the brain of the victim that I was working on, the same sensation happened. I got messages from those brains. Probably in both cases, the last thing that was freshest in their minds. I synced the audio to prove my point. Freaky isn't it?"

Staring at the screen, Goodall went unusually ashen faced. "You know we can't use this video as evidence, but I'm sure this guy works for the CPD."

"A police officer?"

"The Chicago Police Department are not going to be too happy about this, I can tell you. We are supposed to share information. I won't be sharing this."

Goodall sank back into the chair and sat thoughtfully for a few minutes. He was a big hulk of a man, forty-one years old, in great physical condition, well over six feet tall, brown, greying, and short-cropped hair.

"I need a coffee. You OK with getting a drink down town? I'm buying. I need to get a handle on this thing. Burn me a copy of the video on a stick and let's get out of here."

This was the first time anyone had asked Reuben to have a drink with him and he was quite startled by it. Quietly he burned the file to a memory stick, handed it to Goodall and they both left the building.

Goodall drove an old Porsche - a classic collector's car. He had painstakingly restored it to near new condition. The upholstery was immaculate and the engine sounded as sweet as a rocket ship on its way to Mars. It was the first time Reuben had ever been in a Porsche, and even though he wasn't that much interested in cars, he felt the thrill of the speed as Goodall put his foot down and was soon outside his favorite all-night diner. *Henry's* was about three blocks from the morgue and the welcoming neon sign boasted the best burgers in town.

Goodall made straight for the counter stool with Reuben in tow following meekly behind. It was not something Reuben ever did, but he was with his beloved boss and that was all that mattered in the world.

"Hey Steve, a bit early for you, isn't it?" said Henry smiling warmly.

Henry was a plumpish small man with tufts of red hair that peeped out from beneath his cooking hat. A white apron, that had seen better days, was loosely tied around his ample stomach and a teatowel was casually draped over his shoulder. He shuffled from the hot plates to the brewing coffee maker and deposited two steaming cups in front of the men. There were three other people eating burgers at one of the tables. They were absorbed in their eating, and barely seemed to notice Reuben and Goodall enter the diner.

"Yeah, but if I told you why, I'd have to shoot you," Goodall laughed amiably back at him. It was obvious that they knew each other very well. "One of your toasted cheese buns would be nice too."

"Coming up."

"You want anything?" Goodall asked Reuben.

"Starving, actually. Haven't eaten in a couple of days."

"Henry, put on one of your special burgers for my friend," called out Goodall.

"Sure thing Steve."

Reuben was smart enough to know that even though his boss had called him a friend, they were from two very different planets. He liked the thought of it though.

Goodall's friendliness as he turned to face Reuben was replaced with an earnest enquiring look.

"You say you just placed your hands on the brain?"

"That's right."

"Amazing! You realize no-one will ever believe you. I'm not sure I do. If anyone else had told me this, I most certainly wouldn't have."

The food arrived and Reuben fell upon it ravenously

"That was the best! Any chance for another?"

"Henry, you have a fan!" called out Goodall. "Another burger, please."

"Coming up."

Goodall noticed that the three diners had got up, paid their bill and wandered out into the semi-deserted street. He and Reuben were the only people left in *Henry's*.

Goodall took off his beanie. Speaking conspiratorially, so that he could be sure Henry couldn't overhear, he took Reuben by surprise.

"How about you try your party trick on me?"

Obedient as ever, Reuben cleaned his greasy hands with a napkin. Leaning towards Steve, he gently placed them on his boss's head.

A multitude of sensations assaulted Reuben. There were so many, in quick succession, that he had trouble in picturing them all. Among all the jumble, one face stood out; one of the morgue staff, a tall, trendy looking woman, who Reuben had met when he first joined the DA's office. Her name? He wracked his brains. Ah, yes . . . Cynthia Jones.

"Get anything?" asked Goodall, almost wishing he hadn't instigated this interaction.

"You got a lot going on Boss, but the clearest thing I saw was your concern that Cynthia is pregnant and you didn't know how to tell your wife."

"Shit!" exclaimed Goodall, a look of bewilderment on his face "You've convinced me!"

Henry arrived with the second burger and refilled both their coffee mugs. He gave Goodall a very strange querying look but knew he shouldn't make a wise-crack or comment, so scurried off.

"You really saw all that?"

Reuben simply nodded as his mouth was full of burger. There was nothing more to be said anyway. Reuben could see by the steely clench of Goodall's jaw that his boss had heard enough and had no desire to further pursue any more revelations.

"You're coming into the field as a full detective. We are going to blow this town apart! What do you say to that?" joked Goodall, trying to deflect what had been for him a most uncomfortable situation.

Having cleared his plate and wiped his mouth, Reuben slurped his coffee and thought for a while.

"Boss, while I appreciate what you are saying, I'm not

sure about it. Apart from my chess games and my work in the lab, there is not a lot going on in my world. So I don't have much to store, memory wise, in my brain. But once I get into the real world, the amount of data going through my brain will make it harder and harder to isolate any important information. I just did that now because I needed to prove to you I could do it. When I …"

"Reuben, enough! I hear you. Let me worry about that side of it."

There was no way Goodall wanted to get trapped into an hour long dissertation with Reuben. Not at this time of the morning. Not anytime.

"OK, you may be right about this data flow thing and it may well be that you will spend longer in your office on the post-production process, but I think you have a gift we should utilize," Goodall said glaring at Reuben. "And not another word about Cynthia, OK?"

"Of course."

As Goodall laid a twenty-dollar bill on the counter and started to get up, Henry came over and slapped Reuben on the shoulder. Reuben was totally unprepared for the sensation that vibrated through his body and although he tried to conceal it, he felt his shoulders involuntarily tense.

"Nice to meet you too. Anyone who loves my burgers must be alright. Come back again," said Henry winking at Goodall.

"I did love your burgers," whispered Reuben quite nervously. He was not used to speaking to people he didn't know. He was also not used to be being touched by another human.

Once back in the car Goodall smiled at Reuben like an indulgent parent would do when their child had done something special or was about to.

"So, anything you can tell me about Henry? I saw you shake when he touched you."

"Henry was robbed at gunpoint two weeks ago and yesterday he lost two hundred and fifty dollars in a poker game," said Reuben somewhat smugly. He was getting used to the idea that every small bit of info really impressed his boss.

"Well, how about that!"

The ride back to the morgue was swift and silent. Reuben savoured this small window of time with Goodall.

"Thank you very much, Boss. Great car and great food. See you on Monday I guess?"

"Monday, for sure. You have a great weekend," said Goodall as he revved the engine of his Porsche and was out of sight in the blink of an eye.

Reuben walked slowly across the road to his apartment and, after riffling briefly through the mound of mail which had been thrust under his front door, he went into the bathroom, stripped off, and reveled in a long hot shower. The routine kicked in and he was asleep in his bed for six hours before he knew it.

Right on twelve his regular can of sardines on a dry cracker, washed down with a piping hot tea, constituted lunch. The mail was next. Seven brochures of various merchants in the area, four generic letters he termed as junk which he threw in the general vicinity of his paper collection box, and two bills. One bill was from his accountant regarding an overdue tax preparation fee and the other from the IRS informing him where the next tax papers were to be sent.

Reuben fired up his PC, immediately paid his accountant, electronically, and then sent the fellow an email to let him know it had been done and to inform him of the communication from the IRS. Reuben had never met his accountant in person in the five years he employed his services. The man was recommended by the morgue as trustworthy, discreet and predominantly electronic. Exactly what an accountant should be, Reuben had thought at the time, and the arrangement he had suited them both. Except when Reuben purposely forgot to pay his account to gain the extra ten dollars and thirty cents from the interest.

While still at the computer, Reuben had a thought. Why not play detective and see if he could discover more about the police officer he had imaged in his brain and who he actually was. He tried trawling through a photo gallery from the *Chicago Tribune*. Next he tried googling the Chicago Police Department to see what was reported online photographically.

It was arduous trawling without getting any success at all. Websites, newspapers on line, missing person's reports, all had other people's photo and not the cop Reuben was looking for. By eight PM, Reuben was itching to be out of his apartment and back in the relative safety of his office. At ten past eight he bolted over to it.

Using his special ID from the DA's Office, Reuben went into The Chicago Police Department personnel records and continued his earlier search. He was on a mission like a dog looking for the bone he'd lost someplace.

Many of the policemen looked so similar. After looking at countless faces, Reuben was beginning to get confused and was about to give up when one face caught his attention. There was no mistaking it; this was the man Reuben had seen. According to the accompanying personnel profile, Captain Mark Hamilton was thirty-eight years old, twice decorated for bravery under fire, and after completing military service in San Diego received an honourable discharge. He had currently been fifteen years with the police department and was married to wife Emily with two children, Jake, fifteen, and Shari, thirteen.

"His life looks more normal than mine," muttered Reuben to himself. "I wonder what his real story is."

Some people are not always what they appear, thought Reuben. Under the guise of normality, this Mark Hamilton must be a man to be respected and feared. Certainly not to be taken lightly or at face value.

Feeling momentarily guilty that he had gone beyond the brief of his job description and ventured onto Goodall's turf, Reuben thought better of it and exited the police department website. That was that for tonight's amateur detective work.

Opening chess.com, a site where you could play human opponents as well as machines, Reuben went back to his other ongoing chess game. Sitting transfixed, he studied the board for hours without even contemplating a move. The person he was playing had the user name Vercingetorix. The profile that said he was a male and living in Sacramento,

California. The main reason Reuben had selected him was because of the unique game name which Reuben himself had also considered using before he had settled on his other hero from antiquity of about eight hundred years later, Charlemagne.

Strangely, Reuben had labored over his final choice of name for quite a few weeks before basing his final decision on the fact that Charlemagne had lived twice as long as Vercingetorix. Reuben was a secret history buff, and enjoyed contemplating the glories of heroes of the past.

The real Vercingetorix came from the Auvergne region in old France around the modern town of Clermont-Ferrand. He was a giant of a man, well over six feet seven inches tall, broad shoulders, a skilled and fearless warrior and a true leader of the Gauls. Up against the might of the Romans, led by the legendary general Julius Caesar, Vercingetorix won a great victory at The Battle of Gergovia in 52 BCE. Vercingetorix's aim was to unite all the Gallic tribes so that they remained focused on the common enemy, Rome. Caesar's secret treaty deals with local tribes led to Vercingetorix's defeat at the Battle of Alesia in 51BCE. To save his men, Vercingetorix surrendered to the Romans who held him captive for five years after which he was executed in Rome. Reuben considered any online opponent taking the name of such a warrior, would surely be a worthy adversary.

Charlemagne, on the other hand, was widely known as "The Father of Europe" having never been defeated in battle and crowned Emperor. Charlemagne was a hero, trying to fulfill the destiny of his grandfather, who united most of Europe for a period of time. Charlemagne knew how to make deals with the right people at the right time. He was a man who had his finger on the pulse and switched camps whenever he saw a better opportunity. As wily as a cat on heat. For someone of Reuben's nature, here was a man to admire, and maybe aspire to have some of his qualities.

Within chess.com there were notepads so opponents could "chat" with each other but neither Vercingetorix nor Reuben had taken any advantage of them. This game had now been in progress for just over six months and it had been Reuben's turn for a very long time. It was only their second game. The previous encounter had ended in a stalemate and when the offer came for a rematch it was too irresistible to refuse.

Reuben had analyzed every move that he and Vercingetorix had made in their first match to detect any predictable reactions to certain piece placements. Every now and then he would split the screen with the old game and compare the strategies. Probably Vercingetorix was doing the same thing. *How predictable am I*, thought Reuben.

Time had no meaning or relevance to Reuben as the hours flittered away. Every now and then he would take a walk down the deserted corridors to give his legs some respite and exercise from his usual position at the computer.

Without windows in his office, there were no light variations. In this way he proved the theory to himself that humans don't require sleep as regularly as they take it or think they need it. Reuben could spend days glued to a screen and not think anything of it. Work, pleasure and play were all jumbled into one category and they were all in one place - his office. So, for Reuben, when he was safely esconsed in his office, there was no other place he yearned to be. If a bed and shower could be set up in the morgue for him, then life could not be more perfect. Reuben had no interest in females, or males. He was not one of the eighty percent of males who, according to research, spent sixty percent of their time thinking about women. In this way, along with his minimal and irregular sleeping hours, Reuben was far more productive with his time than anyone else at the morgue.

Reuben was actually considering a chess move when a doctor in a white suit entered his office. Reuben realised to his astonishment that it was Monday morning and he'd survived another weekend. In the doctor's hand was an enclosed cyclinder, no doubt with another body part. Reuben became suddenly alert, focusing on the cylinder to see if he could guess what was in it. The doctor sensed his concentrated gaze.

"All that was left from a house fire. Don't know anything more than that. See what you can make of it," said the doctor and abruptly left.

"Will do," Reuben called after the man.

If anyone had asked Reuben what the doctor who made the delivery to him looked like, Reuben would not be able to give a full description, as he never made eye contact with the man and made a point of not communicating with him other than what was absolutely necessary. The niceties of hello, goodbye and thanks were rare. Reuben would not have made a good witness in any court of law had he been asked to identify the doctor. He never really saw anyone for that matter (except maybe his beloved Goodall).

Reuben opened a fresh packet of rubber gloves and slipped on the latex as easy as pie. Finding the human remains among the ash in the cylinder was the real challenge, but Reuben saw it immediately - a fragment no bigger than a large breadcrumb. It was definitely bone and Reuben had to determine whether it was animal or human remains and where it fitted into the anatomy.

Even in funeral pyres and crematorium ceremonies there were, invariably, pieces of the skeleton that avoided total incineration from the massive heat generated to burn the bodies. In those cases, attendants would sift through the ash for fragments that they would then crush into a powder and pour back into the ash. Looking for gold and silver that had been melted down, as well as precious stones, was a bonus incentive to do this task thoroughly. Quite a nice business had built up in some countries living off the residues of others.

The workhorse, The KL33, was a machine that been around for twenty or so years. Real state-of-the-art, at that time anyway, for analyzing anything and coming up with suggestions to follow up. Reuben was very familiar with every facet of its operation and correctly second-guessed it on several occasions. Like all things, Reuben considered what he did as a game of sorts whereby a problem would be delivered and a solution was required to be found. Reuben's game opponents also extended to the KL33 as he was determined to prove, if only to himself, that he could be ultimately smarter than it was. It's only a machine, he would say to himself.

The machine beeped to indicate it had completed the analysis, giving a few options. Just as Reuben had presupposed, the remnant was human and came from the shinbone area of either a male or female. The fibia was ruled out and the only other conclusion was the tibia. Being such a small, irregular, piece of bone, there was no way to ascertain the exact position it must have once slotted into and this annoyed Reuben. He was a perfectionist. He didn't like incomplete solutions. In this particular case he had no choice but to go through the basics and record them in his report.

> Ash fragments on and around the fragment of tibia indicate that the bone was exposed to a great heat. DNA testing has revealed blood type was O, bone density was abnormally low. First up opinion is that the victim was suffering from a disease that was probably incurable. Leukemia or one of a number of cancerous maladies come to mind. No gender could be identified. Date of death was approximately two days before this examination.

Reuben emailed his report to the general DA's address knowing it would be seen reasonably quickly. No point in phoning direct to Special Agent Goodall. Not really a lot to base any major crime investigation on. Reuben carefully put the bone fragment back in its cylinder and deposited it in the refrigerated dispatch filing cabinet. He noted that nothing had been retrieved from the cabinet for the last month. Unconcerned, Reuben went back to his chess match.

He got close to making a move a couple of times but somehow talked himself out of it. Trying to outthink an opponent like Vercingetorix was proving complex as Reuben generally projected six possible moves ahead. Holding it in his brain and retrieving the moves as required was the real skill. Staring at the screen seemed to be the only safe move, if one could call that a move.

Goodall knocked as he entered Reuben's office. Reuben immediately minimized the game to show the official DA screen shot, a huge logo with Latin inscriptions.

"Busy?" enquired Goodall.

"Just finished, actually. Another job?"

"Of sorts. I'm doing a press conference at The Chicago Police Department Head Office and would like you to tag along."

"Will he be there?"

"I sure hope so." Goodall's tight-lipped smile indicated he could be plotting something. "They said he would."

As he always did when vacating his office, Reuben went into his routine, methodically switching off the computers and neatly filing away the papers and notepads. It was as if what happened in the future with Reuben might not include him ever getting back to his beloved sanctuary and he wanted it in the most pristine condition possible in case of that unlikely eventuality.

The drive down to South Michigan Avenue was as exciting for Reuben as the ride to *Henry's* had been a couple of days earlier. The Porsche clung to the road like a cat as it sped through one red light after another with some gay abandonment of the road rules. Goodall, of course, knew the way. He also knew when and where to flaunt his skills.

Any traffic patrol officer witnessing it would know this car belonged to the DA's department and would not bother to report it in with the useless paperwork that was required. What would be the point?

Reuben followed Special Agent Goodall into the noticeably plush area that was set aside for press conferences within the Chicago Police Department. Goodall directed Reuben to sit by the entrance, speak to no-one and just be an observer. Reuben obediently plopped himself down, as instructed, and did a mental count of the forty-three people there. Some were in uniform but most not. Reuben soon spotted Captain Mark Hamilton seated near the podium. Nothing out of the ordinary. A nice blue suit pretty much the same as Goodall's.

A very attractive woman sat next to him, but Reuben could not detect any conversation between them. This woman was striking. Long blond hair that fell innocently over her pale green outfit. Totally surprising himself with an unprecedented feeling, Reuben found himself experiencing something that he could only define, from his limited knowledge, as lust and envy. Here was a goddess who could have had her pick of the room, if she wished to. She was totally out of Reuben's league. Oh how he wished it were not so. His daydream extended to his parents' Friday night ritual dinners and what his mother would say or think if he brought such a woman in as his partner. The daydream came to an abrupt end as he managed to catch the last few lines of his boss's speech

"Vigilance is the key at this moment, officers. The opportunities that organized crime have given to certain of our members throughout the country are short-sighted Certainly not worth the consequences if matters end up in a court of law. I need to reinforce this message as my colleagues are also doing in other states. In closing I sincerely wish you all well in the fight for law and order. Keep up the good work."

The round of applause really only reflected a level of relief from most of the audience as to the generality of the speech, and that the lecture was over. There were no specifics. For everyone, nothing had changed. In fact the very reason it was deemed as so important to the ones that were ordered to attend mystified them.

The handful of journalists present also looked somewhat underwhelmed, wondering why they had wasted their time on a general speech probably devised only to placate the powers that be, and assure the mayor the CPD was still on the case fighting the good fight against organized crime.

The blond bombshell passed Reuben as she made a quick exit and he caught a whiff of some fragrance, like musk, as she left. Goodall made his way quickly to Reuben in time to intercept Hamilton as he headed for the door.

"Captain, I'd like to introduce you to one of our analysts, Reuben Cohn. Reuben, Captain Mark Hamilton."

"Pleased to meet you sir," said Reuben extending his hand.

"Thank you for that," said Hamilton, shaking hands with Reuben.

"A very fine speech. Very fine," said Hamilton, winking at Goodall. Without further banter, he was off like a greyhound at the races. Goodall eyed him all the way and then indicated to Reuben that they should leave as well.

"Let's go!"

Once inside the Porsche, Goodall leaned over and expectantly faced Reuben.

"Anything to report?"

"I'm not a hundred percent sure as there was a lot of garbage circulating but I did get a name that was pretty clear."

"And that name was?" asked Goodall quite impatiently.

"Domenicci. Albert Domenicci. Does it mean anything to you, Boss?"

"Oh yes it does," said Goodall quite calmly. "Alfredo's son, Alberto. I really thought that family was through when Alfredo was killed. Maybe not. Maybe not."

Goodall revved up the Porsche and it didn't take long before the familiar facade of the morgue came into view.

"Did you glean anything from anyone else in the Police Department?"

"Only that blond in the front row."

"Hannah Martin. She is top shelf alright. Detective too I might add," chuckled Goodall as he pulled the car to a halt outside the morgue. "A little out of your league, I would suggest."

"I had the same thought too," said Reuben as he scrambled awkwardly out of the Porsche and waved as it sped off.

On getting back to his office, Reuben noticed that his door was slightly ajar. Someone had been in there. He quickly checked the dispatch filing cabinet to find that it had finally been cleared. Conflicting thoughts bombarded

Reuben's mind. He was definitely happy that the fridge had been cleared, but suddenly a fresh realisation sprang to the fore. After listening to what little he'd heard of Goodall's monologue on organized crime and police involvement, Reuben worried that there were people around who had clearance to get into The Cook County Morgue; people who could actually be a future threat to him. Reuben had never considered police officers as anything more than servants of the people working as team players with the DA's Department. He thought differently about the police now.

He felt differently about himself too. There was an air of confidence and a sense of worth that he had never experienced before. There was also a willingness to express himself in brief dialogue with other humans. He was still a dork, still on the spectrum, but he now knew what he aspired to be. Worthy of someone like Hannah Martin.

The rest of Monday was eventless. Reviewing completed audio files, hoping to extract something more, proved fruitless, so around four o'clock Reuben gave up. He locked up his office, braved the windy street back to his apartment, showered and went straight to bed. He was soon sound asleep and dreaming of Hannah Martin.

It felt a bit strange to be going to the office at a "normal" time as Reuben made it to his office right on nine. A note on his desk indicated that a delivery had been made and was awaiting his analysis. He retrieved the canister from the cabinet, placed it on his desk and stared blankly at it. For some reason, going through his normal procedures felt like a task he didn't want to do at that moment. Guilt was his main motivator as he gloved up and unscrewed the container. A small bone fragment awaited his attention. He worked through the basics, finding nothing special, but lacking his usual enthusiasm. Some part of him seemed to be unusually distracted and working on auto-pilot.

Vercingetorix awaited as Reuben logged into the chess game again and got himself up to speed regarding the possibility of a move. The board looked different even though Reuben instinctively knew that nothing had been altered. He was still at a loss to fully comprehend his unfamiliar state of mind when Goodall knocked and entered his office.

"Good morning Reuben," he said and smiled when he saw the chess game on the screen. "Busy?"

"Not that busy," said Reuben as he minimized the screen, "as you can see."

"Are you ever going to make another move?"

"My head's not in it at the moment. What's happening?"

"There was a murder on the East Side on Sunday morning and this kid turns up at the local police station and confesses to it," said Goodall sitting down and facing Reuben. "I don't buy it."

"Has this person confessed to crimes before?" asked Reuben.

"Not to my knowledge. The weird part about it is his description of the crime scene is pretty much word for word to what the crime detective's was."

"You are being pressured by the Mayor to get a conviction

happening but something tells you he doesn't fit the profile of your everyday killer?"

"Well, yes."

"You'd like me to interview him and see what I can glean from it?"

"If you're interested."

"I could go with a change. I'll give it a go."

"Great. Let's do it then before the system swallows him up."

Twenty minutes of Porsche riding had Reuben secretly wishing he could learn to drive one of those beasts. The East Side looked a lot cleaner and up-market than where the morgue was situated. A very modern-looking police station sported bland but pleasant photographs and oil paintings adorned the walls. Not at all like the bleak starkness of other stations Reuben had been shown when he joined the DA's Department. It smelled of wealth, privilege and power.

Goodall had requested that the young man who had confessed be brought to the interview room for a final assessment before accepting his admission of guilt. From the Porsche to the room took all of four minutes and a scrawny man of about twenty was marched in and sat down. The man's name was Mason McWillis, according to his file, and he lived very close to the station. About six feet tall with peroxide-dyed hair that sneaked out from under his baseball cap. Reuben studied the file and then purposely got up from his chair and stood next to Mason extending his hand.

"My name is Reuben Cohn and I'm with the DA's office.

Are they treating you well?"

"Ok," said Mason making a real effort through his handcuffs to shake Reuben's hand.

Reuben turned to one of the officers. "Could you uncuff him please? I will take full responsibility."

The officer looked over at Goodall who gave a thumbs-up signal, and then the officer glanced at the one-way glass mirror to the detective on the other side. The officer reluctantly uncuffed Mason with a scowl on his face as he stepped back into the corner of the room with his left hand firmly on his service revolver.

"Mason, could you stand up for me?" asked Reuben quietly.

It appeared that Mason was enjoying the attention and the theatrics that he supposed were in store for him during the forthcoming interview. With an almost smug expression on his face, Mason stood up, pushing the chair back with a scraping sound. Reuben, who was about the same size as Mason, quite unexpectedly gave the young man a bear hug and held him tightly for a few seconds. Mason was bewildered and struggled to break free. To his amazement, Reuben whispered in his ear.

"Mason, you are the victim here, not a murderer. Your father has been molesting and raping you since you were eight years old and you thought that this was a way for it to end, didn't you?"

Any signs of smugness instantly dissolved, as Mason's body crumpled and tears sprang to his eyes. "I didn't tell anybody! I didn't tell anybody!" cried Mason, as Reuben released his bear-hug.

"I know you didn't. Don't you think it is about time you did?"

Mason fell back into his chair and sobbed uncontrollably for a good five minutes while Reuben gently patted him on the shoulder.

"I'm assuming that you have a police radio receiver at home and when you heard the report you memorized it, didn't you?"

Mason looked up sadly and nodded resignedly while wiping the tears from his eyes.

"I didn't tell anybody."

"Why don't you write it all down and I promise you that the abuse and the nightmares will stop. It will all be over."

Reuben motioned to the officer in the room to bring a pad and pen so that a new statement could be made.

Just as Mason began writing his story, the detective who had been watching the unexpected outcome, entered the room. Much to Reuben's surprise it was Hannah Martin. Reuben became instantly nervous and jittery in her presence.

"Good work sir, whoever you are," she said extending her hand to Reuben.

"Reuben Cohn," he said taking her hand gingerly, unable to look her directly in the eye.

"Reuben Cohn, why are you acting as if you are guilty of something? What do you have to be guilty of?" she laughed.

Reuben took away his hand and went over to the desk. He pulled out a little pad and wrote, *You are in a lot of trouble*, and thrust the note into the hand of Hannah Martin so that no-one would notice. Most eyes were on Mason as he sobbed and continued writing his story. Goodall walked over to Reuben with a fatherly smile.

"Time for us to leave, I'd say."

Without looking at Mason or Hannah, Reuben and Goodall made their way back to the Porsche.

"Good work Reuben. I knew my instincts about this kid not being the one were right."

"Thanks Boss."

Reuben considered telling Goodall about what he had learnt when Hannah Martin shook hands with him and that he had slipped her a note too. But Goodall sped off making that a decision to be put on hold. It was hard to tell if Goodall had seen the transaction and was biding his time on it. Reuben assessed that he hadn't. She was a stunningly good-looking woman and the chemistry, within Reuben anyway, was so fresh and raw that he already felt a divided loyalty and a little confused as to what he would do next if she ever made contact. He didn't have to wait long. Exactly an hour later she appeared at his office door.

Hannah Martin was the type of beautiful woman you would expect to see on the cover of a film or TV magazine, not as a tough homicide detective. Mid-twenties, five foot seven, stylish clothes that fitted perfectly over her shapely body. She was armed and dangerous in many ways.

"Your note intrigued me," she said warmly as she slid into his office and planted herself in a chair. She looked completely relaxed, with a near-genuine smile that suggested all sorts of things.

There was no doubt she knew how good she looked and that most red-blooded American men would fall over themselves to please her or be in the same room as her.

"Having you doing ten to fifteen years in a prison is surprisingly of some concern to me," said Reuben nervously.

"What exactly do you mean?"

"I'll ask you some questions and I'll also give you the answers if you like?"

"I'm listening," she said as the sexy smile she had worn on entering Reuben's office disappeared.

"Did you know that Captain Mark Hamilton is the prime suspect in a murder investigation? No! Did you know that he has a plan to implicate you and let you take the rap for it? No! I know you didn't do it but did you know that we know all about Alberto Domenicci? I suspect not! Did you know that I am stepping over a line in order to save you? No! Well you do now, don't you?" Shaking, and pausing for breath, Reuben found himself as shocked by his outburst as Hannah obviously was.

"That was quite a speech," she said grimly, "and who exactly are you to be telling me all this? You'd make a great crime writer, you know. How in God's name did you come up with this convoluted plot?"

Reuben was saved from answering her question by his mobile phone which started to ring. He nervously gestured to Hannah, indicating she should stay.

"Excuse me, it's my mother."

Hannah mouthed, "It's OK."

"Hello Mum, everything alright?"

"Yes dear, just inviting you for Friday night if you are free?"

"Sounds good and I might bring a friend too if that's alright?"

"Yes dear, anyone we know?"

"I'm in a meeting now, see you at six on Friday, 'bye."

Reuben hung up the phone and looked across at Hannah Martin with a glint in his eyes, as if a great joke was about to be entered into.

"Dinner with my parents at six on Friday if you are free?"

"Me?" Hannah looked incredulous.

"Pick me up at five as I don't own a car and haven't learnt to drive as yet. Does that work for you?"

Reuben amazed even himself by this most forward approach he was taking with this woman he barely knew, who had quite unexpectedly and disproportionately become a focus in his most uneventful life. He was on a roll and couldn't stop himself.

"It should be kind of funny having you on my arm for the evening. It will get them off my back with their noodering about finding a good Jewish girl to settle down with," he blurted nervously.

After a few moments of stunned silence in which Reuben feared that he had over-stepped the mark, Hannah finally responded.

"I can do that for you. What is it that you precisely do for the DA's office anyway?" she asked.

"I'm a dull and boring analyst. That's it, I'm afraid."

"Hazardous business, I'd say," she said with a sexy smile returning to her face. "Certainly not boring to me."

"Friday then?"

"Friday is locked in."

As Hannah closed the door behind her, Reuben's office returned to normal - just him and the computers. But his safe haven now felt abnormally empty and changed. It was as if all of the tectonic plates had moved around him and he was now stranded somewhere and in some place that he had never contemplated being before.

Reuben spent the rest of the day machinating his next move with Vercingetorix as well as nervously contemplating what to say to his boss. Neither questions seemed to proffer up an easy answer. Both would have to wait.

Back at his apartment that evening, Reuben performed one of his annual cleans. Papers that had been strewn in crevices were binned and the dust on the windows and blinds was sprayed and wiped. His bed was another matter. Six months since he had changed the sheets was quite normal, but deep down he now felt grubby and a little embarrassed that he lived like he did. It was confusing. Things seemed to be changing, and it appeared that his days as a mole could be coming to an end too.

As Reuben opened his office door next morning he was startled to find Special Agent Steve Goodall waiting for him there.

"Boss!"

"I understand you had a visitor yesterday, according to the register. Anything to report?" he asked cagily.

"Oh yes indeed I did. Not just a visitor either. Hannah Martin."

"I know. What did she want?"

"Insurance, I believe."

Reuben let the words resonate with a silence. Goodall allowed it and left Reuben the space to explain.

"I told her Mark Hamilton was under investigation and he might try to set her up. She took the bait. There is no doubt in my mind that she was present when Hamilton fired the gun but was too afraid to do anything about it. I've offered to assist by turning her into an inside informer and she is considering it."

Reuben enjoyed the attention his boss was giving him, even though his reporting of the truth was beginning to be a little stretched. For added effect he threw in the surprising date he'd organized.

"We're having dinner at my parents' place on Friday to nut out the details."

"You and Hannah Martin!" laughed Goodall. "I told you, you would be a good detective didn't I?"

"Maybe. It seemed like too good an opportunity to become friends with her, get her out of a fix and be of some use to The Department. What do you think?"

"And exactly when were you going to let me in on it?"

"After Friday, regardless of what decision she comes to."

"Hannah Martin. You are a bit of a dark horse aren't you? Can't say I blame you but you're not the same Reuben I took to *Henry's* a few days ago. I like what I'm hearing. Run with it and keep me in the loop."

"Thanks Boss, I hoped you might see it that way too. It's all about usable evidence isn't it?"

"You bet it is," said Goodall with a wry grin on his face as he realized he was hearing his own words back at him. Goodall made his way out of the office wondering what he had uncorked in the new Reuben.

"I know I've changed," muttered Reuben to himself, as he began speculating what on earth could be giving rise to these noticeable personality modifications he was experiencing.

I'll bet that all these years I've been missing some elements in my brain and it made me the nerd I was. Now, I've picked up the street wise canny from the alley cat and gleaned all sorts of stuff from the people I've been in close contact with. I am in a state of evolution that bears little resemblance to my old self. It did get me a date with Hannah Martin though. What else will I navigate into? I have to be as vigilant as ever and always on my guard.

Abandoning this perplexing line of thought, he turned his computer on and went straight to his chess game.

Reuben felt a rush of blood as he entered a move against Vercingetorix. Queen from f6 to h4. Having played his move, Reuben calmly turned the game off, even though it was still active in cyberspace. He then decided to follow a hunch by accessing The Internal Revenue Service site in Washington DC.

After typing in his DA's clearance password, Reuben typed in Albert Domenicci and took a look at his tax statement for the past year. From the facts online, Reuben began to glean information about Domenicci. It appeared the man owned a business that imported olive oil from only one supplier in Sicily, La Fattorio del Popolo or The People's

Farm. He then onsold the entire shipment equally to two wholesale companies, Sunshine Oil and Sicilian Oil.

Reuben then looked at the IRS statements for both those companies. He found nothing irregular in their turnover figures. Sicilian Oil was a four-man enterprise with other products and clients all over the States. Sunshine Oil was a much bigger organization that owned several offshoot companies in different areas. They also had other products that they repackaged and sold. Nothing looked out of the ordinary.

Reuben looked into all of the twenty offshoot companies and made notes about each one. He proceeded to research each of those companies too but again found nothing out of the ordinary. The companies included moderately successful enterprises in brickworks, glassworks, real estate, nightclubs, water distillery, trucking transport and several junk yards.

Pulling up the statements showing Domenicci's profit for the past ten years, Reuben discovered it had been, give or take, $100,000 per year. He then compared the wholesale rate of the bottled oil on the open marketplace and found it very competitive. Squeaky clean in fact. Domenicci's wholesale price to his suppliers had not changed much during that 10-year period even though the freight and import had increased by a small margin. *Was Domenicci simply being a good businessman by wearing the difference and still managing to make a moderate income?* thought Reuben. Certainly everything appeared legal but not enough turnover to have police officers on his payroll. *Why would he need them? How is he generating the big dollars?*

Friday could not have come earlier. At a quarter to five, Reuben locked up his office and, breaking with his usual modus operandus, exited the building via the front door. His heart beat a little faster as he waited for his date. Right on five o'clock, driving a brand new navy blue Ford that had been souped up for police activities, there she was. Reuben got in the car as coolly as if he were an old hand at it.

"I like punctuality. How are you?" asked Reuben sneaking a sideways glance at Hannah.

"So do I. You can tell a lot about a person when they make an appointment for a time and then keep it," she replied.

"And you also know a lot about a person by who they know. Do you happen to know Albert Domenicci?" asked Reuben calmly.

"Of course! Everyone knows he's a notable crime figure."

"Without wishing to seem too forward, can I ask, have you ever taken money from him?"

Hannah made no attempt to disguise her shock at the impertinence of the question. "What sort of a question is that? Of course not! Why would you even ask?"

Ignoring her question, he countered with, "Could I see your hands for a moment?"

"Strange request but ok," she said offering them to him.

Reuben took her hands tightly in his, trying to disassociate himself from their softness, and focus upon the signals he began to receive. He'd never even held a woman's hand, so overcoming the obvious distraction was quite a challenge.

The signals only confirmed what Reuben already suspected.

"You know, you shouldn't lie to me? We already know you have and still do. Try to be more honest with me, as it will benefit you in the long run."

Swallowing her fury at his outrageous impertinence, she asked matter-of-factly, "Why on earth are you helping me?"

"Well for starters you are the most beautiful woman I have ever seen. There, I've said it. And I don't really know anything more other than you look lovely tonight and thanks for coming too."

Ignoring the compliment, Hannah was totally at a loss as to what was motivating this peculiar man. It had become all too obvious to her that Reuben and the DA's office knew all about the dealings between Domenicci and certain members of the upper echelons of the CPD. The façade of denial seemed pointless. "It's true that a few of us are involved in helping Domenicci to protect his enterprises . . ."

"Let's not discuss it right now, alright?" interrupted Reuben. "You changed your perfume from the other day?" he added with a sly smile.

Again Hannah felt at a loss to second-guess what would come out of Reuben's mouth next. Playing along seemed the best course of action.

"I usually wear Poison to work and after work is Jean Paul Gaultier. You approve?"

"You know I do," smiled Reuben like a puppy-dog panting at every word from its master.

Reuben's parents lived on Sycamore Street, a leafy suburb of Vernon Hills, just under an hour's drive from the morgue. Reuben had Hannah put the address into her GPS tracker and he noted that her style of driving was decidedly different from that of Goodall's. She was slower, and careful not to break any of the road rules.

The traffic was a bit congested. Hannah had put the radio on quietly in the background with some soft jazz emanating from it. Reuben enjoyed every minute even though he now found himself incapable of making any further meaningful conversation with her.

Reuben was reluctant to point out that the house they had just pulled up in front of was in fact his old family home. The house was mostly old style with a lot of timber, which needed a new paint job. It was very different to the more modern brick dwellings on either side of it, but it had an old-world charm that was now being lost on Reuben as he saw the house through new eyes and wondered what Hannah thought of it. He didn't have to wonder for long.

"Thanks heavens not all the charming old 1930s homes have been bulldozed in the rush to modernize this city," observed Hannah.

Reuben wanted to stay in the car with Hannah but was smart enough to play out the charade as he had planned it.

A rose garden with an archway marked the start of a little gravel pathway, lined with flower beds, that led to the solid oak front door. Reuben had a key and ushered Hannah inside.

"Hi Mum, Dad, I'm home!" called out Reuben.

"Come in dear," called back his mother from the kitchen.

Reuben led Hannah through a narrow hallway that was filled with family memorabilia from all eras. Reuben's father, Jacob, had served in Lebanon during the Civil War and his photo in full uniform stood out from the rest. Hannah immediately noticed how much Reuben resembled his father.

"This must be your father," she said pointing to it.

"That's Dad in all his glory. It's our own walk of memories. That's Mum when she was a nurse and the kid in most of them is me. You really are a detective."

"No brothers or sisters?"

"I think when I came onto the scene they really didn't want another like me!"

Reuben ushered Hannah into the dining room area where his father was deep in his newspaper, as always. Jacob was mid-fifties, balding, heavy horn-rimmed glasses that hung loosely on his nose. Hannah thought correctly that he was around five foot seven and a hundred and sixty pounds. She was well trained in that sort of quick assessment of people. He looked up and was quite taken aback to see such a pretty woman with Reuben. To see anyone with him actually.

"Dad, this is Hannah, a work colleague."

"Pleased to meet you sir," said Hannah extending her hand.

"Very surprised, I'd say, to meet you," he said smiling warmly as he shook her hand. "Never met one of Reuben's friends before."

"That would be because I've never had anyone here," cut in Reuben.

Sara, Reuben's mother, came into the room still wearing her apron and embraced Reuben. She was a smidge over five feet, plump, with an open, friendly face and light brown hair that looked as if it had recently been tinted.

"It's been so long, Reuben."

"I know. Sorry. Meet Hannah and watch what you say, she's a homicide detective," laughed Reuben.

"Pleased to meet you Mrs. Cohn and thanks for inviting me."

"Reuben's not in any trouble is he?" enquired Jacob.

"Not at the moment," chuckled Hannah.

Sara did the blessings over the Shabbat candles and Reuben did his best to explain the ritual to Hannah. Jacob held up his glass of wine and performed the traditional Kiddush. He then passed around the cup for everyone to take a sip and handed the plate of challah around so everyone could partake of the symbolic bread.

"It's pretty much like a blessing to God to say thanks for what we have and to be ever mindful that it might all end one day," said Reuben instructionally to Hannah.

"We do something similar when I go home to Oregon on our Sunday lunch after church."

"Same religion. Just a different take on it, I guess," replied Reuben.

"You still go to church here dear?" asked Sara as she started to serve the food around.

"Being in the police force sort of knocked all that out of me, I'm afraid."

"Reuben was training to be a doctor before he quit and joined the government," stated Jacob a little gruffly. "Did you know that?"

"No I didn't," said Hannah, wondering how she'd ever got herself into this situation. The Cohn's seemingly thought there was more between her and her son than the actuality of them barely knowing each other.

Looking over at Sara, she ventured into safe territory. "Delicious food."

During dinner Reuben's mind was on anything but the meal. What exactly was Albert Domenicci's scam and how big was it that he had to pay off the police? A multitude of theories coursed through his mind. One of them seemed like a real possibility and he involuntarily exclaimed.

"That's it! That's got to be the way he is doing it!"

Everyone looked over at him. Especially Hannah.

"Everything alright dear?" asked Sara.

"Oh yes. I was just working on a problem at work is all."

"I've never even known exactly what you do," said Jacob.

"Analysis, Dad. Crunch numbers for the DA."

Reuben plowed into his food like a ravenous dog and Hannah was quite bemused by it all. Sara noticed and shrugged her shoulders with a sigh. Reuben got the uncomfortable vibe that they were staring at him.

"What?"

"Oh nothing dear. I guess you'll never change will you?"

Sara and Hannah shared a conspiratorial smile as Reuben, undeterred, resumed his assault on the food.

At the end of the meal as Reuben and Hannah were leaving, he gave his mum a hug and whispered in her ear.

"Thanks Mum, I'll contact the Veteran Affairs and see if

they can chat to Dad about his violent outbursts towards you. Ok?"

Sara's eyes widened with alarmed disbelief. "How did you find out?"

"It's what I do Mum. I read signs and analyze them. I'll see you later."

Sara felt deeply shocked that somehow Reuben knew what awful things she had been going through of late, but smiled awkwardly and kissed him goodnight. Hannah kissed Sara too and shook hands with Jacob.

"Nice to meet you sir."

"It was a pleasure for me too," said Jacob, smiling approvingly, obviously impressed.

Reuben and his dad acknowledged one another and that was as good as it ever got with them. Jacob sensed that something was different about his son tonight. He couldn't put his finger on it, as he was too set in his rigid opinion of Reuben.

Back in the car, Hannah performed a U-turn and headed homeward.

She had picked up on the vibe between Reuben and his family.

"Your mother seems really nice. Is she under some stress at home with your dad, I wonder?"

"You bet! He is prone to some violent outbursts and I have never interfered or said anything until tonight."

"I noticed."

"You don't miss much do you?"

"It's my job."

Reuben simply nodded and sat back in the seat. It was now or never, he thought, to broach the subject of cooperation and collusion. Hannah noticed his silence and pulled the car into the kerb.

"I guess we need to talk don't we?"

"I've spoken with Special Agent Goodall who you may or may not know."

"Never met him but know who he is from the lecture he gave the other day."

"Well, we can keep your involvement to a minimum and say you were, and still are, acting under-cover for the DA's Department."

"What do I have to do to get that protection?"

"Meet with Goodall and me tomorrow at the morgue and write a report on Captain Mark Hamilton and as much detail as you can regarding the killing and his ongoing involvement with Albert Domenicci."

"That all!" she laughed awkwardly, her internal stress level rising imperceptibly. "No one will work with me again in the CPD you know. They won't trust me not to turn them in too. Not to mention what Alberto will want to do to me when he finds out."

"They won't necessarily have to know," said Reuben very seriously.

"Yeah right!"

"You can trust Goodall, and you know you can trust me. Think about the limb I've gone out on too, and also think about hard prison time. Ex-cops do harder time I've been told."

"Some deal alright. But what choice do I have?"

"You could have all the DA's Department killed by tonight or, for my sake, please do the right thing before it blows up in all our faces. What time can you make it tomorrow? The earlier the better."

"Eight-thirty?"

"Perfect. I'll show you the side entrance so there won't be a record of you on the guard-book."

"I guess I'm in then," she said resignedly.

"Good call, I'd say."

Hannah started up the car again and it seemed from the increased speed, that the weight on her mind was playing out in her driving.

Reuben directed Hannah to the side of the morgue and they parted ways. As she drove away he watched her, thinking, *What in the hell am I getting myself into?*

Reuben dialed his boss. Goodall answered straight away.

"How did your date go, Reuben? Did it go well?" he asked with a hint of sarcasm and maybe envy.

"Very well Boss. Hannah has agreed to write a report and act as a go-between. She will be in my office tomorrow morning at eight-thirty so that you can witness it. Is that alright?"

"I did agree to go shopping with my wife, but she's used to this sort of thing, and it shouldn't take too long. Well done again. You keep surprising and impressing me with your work. The Department needs more good men like you."

"Thank you sir. See you tomorrow."

Reuben felt good all over. Apart from the shock of

learning about his mother's ongoing battle with a war-affected, violent husband, it had been a surprisingly great day. He made a note in his mobile phone diary to contact Veterans Affairs first thing Monday morning. There was no way he was going to neglect this duty. His mother needed protecting and there was no one else who would do it. *Probably lots of women go through the same dramas. Sure hope someone is there for them too,* thought Reuben.

The morgue at eight fifteen in the morning was a rather forbidding looking place. With the morning fog not quite yet dispersed, it had an eerie quality, quite fitting to the business that went on inside.

Before long, Hannah drove up and parked outside. There were no other cars or people around and the air felt a little chilly. Reuben still had the exuberant feeling that here was this goddess prepared to work with him and The Department and that he had arranged it. Life was beginning to be almost perfect. A real relationship was now firmly on his agenda.

"Good morning Hannah," said Reuben extending his hand and trying unsuccessfully to hide his emotions.

"I hope it is," she said shaking his hand firmly.

Terror ripped through every part of Reuben. Even though he was not a fortune teller, knowing the specifics of the future, the dark and menacing thoughts pulsing from Hannah's brain left him in no doubt that she was planning the darker course of action that he had made a joke of a few hours earlier. He coughed violently to conceal his reactions and excused himself.

With his mobile phone in hand he started to text a message to Goodall. Hannah looked at him questioningly.

"Just letting my boss know we are already here," he said in as casual a fashion as he could muster.

Boss, it's a trap. She's planning some sort of hit on us, and the guards. Call the FBI quick and get me some help. I'll stall her in my office. Reuben.

Reuben dialed the combination lock on the door and ushered Hannah to his office. As usual the lights were on and all seemed as peaceful and dead as it always was. Hannah sat down and flashed him one of her trademark smiles.

Already in his car on the way to the meeting, Goodall heard his phone ping. Seeing Reuben's panicked message, he knew what had to be done. He had the number of the morgue's front desk on auto-dial. There was no answer to the call and the phone rang out. Figuring he shouldn't risk police involvement by doing anything more locally, Goodall then phoned the front desk of the FBI in Washington DC.

"Special Agent Steve Goodall from the Chicago District Attorney's Office."

"Yes sir, what can I do for you?"

"We are under attack at the Cook County Morgue. I believe the two front desk officers are down but that is not confirmed, I have an agent inside and will join him presently. Immediate response is required here without the Police Department knowing as I believe they are involved."

"Very good sir, I am alerting a special unit in your area right now. Will keep in contact when we are in position."

"Thank you."

Goodall revved up his Porsche and sped towards the morgue.

"Really nice meeting your parents last night. Thanks for inviting me. Maybe we can do it again sometime?" said Hannah Martin.

"Of course. I'm sure they enjoyed it too."

Smack on eight-thirty, Goodall marched through the door and eyed Hannah up and down suspiciously.

"So you have decided to come across and assist us with our investigations on the Captain Mark Hamilton affair, have you?"

"That's right. I have," she said very formally.

"I'd say that's a pretty wise decision," said Goodall, discreetly slipping his hand inside his suit jacket. Hannah's eyes widened as Goodall took out his Glock 17 service pistol and aimed it at her head. Almost in the same smooth action he took out a pair of handcuffs.

"You make one move towards your weapon and I'll shoot," Goodall said calmly looking at Hannah. "Hands behind your back please."

No stranger to this arrest scenario, Goodall deftly slipped and locked the handcuffs on a startled and upset Hannah.

Reuben suddenly felt himself deeply disappointed to see his romantic plans crumble into dust before his eyes.

Looking directly at Hannah he said angrily, "Why do you always lie to me? I was prepared to save you and yet you chose the wrong way again. Why?"

Despite her apparent dire straits, Hannah had a modicum

of inner confidence that her scheme could still work out and smiled slyly at Reuben.

"When did you know?" she asked him.

"I always knew," lied Reuben. "The FBI is all over the area."

"Really?" she said, her smug look giving way to one of slight worry.

"Just waiting for the all clear," said Goodall as he extracted Hannah's pistol from her shoulder holster. "You won't be needing this anymore," he said handing it to Reuben. "We should be safe to wait inside here."

Hannah was about to say something as Goodall tied his handkerchief around her mouth so that she couldn't utter any warning sounds. Goodall dialed the front door guards again. The phone rang a few times and this time it was answered.

"Front door."

"Special Agent Steve Goodall here. What is your name?"

"Leo Ruiz sir."

"Prepare for the worst then," said Goodall calmly hanging up his phone. Leaning closer to Reuben he whispered, "I know Leo Ruiz's voice and that is not him. It's started alright."

Goodall quickly locked the door and listened for any noise in the corridor that could indicate that an attack was imminent. Hannah had distress written over her beautiful face with beads of perspiration forming on her forehead. Reuben edged behind his desk, sat down in his swivel chair and aimed the gun uncertainly at the door.

Goodall's phone started to beep with an incoming message. He quickly turned the sound off and with a gesture indicated to Reuben to do the same. Quickly complying, Reuben in turn gestured to Hannah. Goodall nodded and, rummaging quickly through Hannah's handbag, found her phone. Knowing he couldn't access the phone, he placed it inside an unused canister within the storage fridge so that any sound coming from it would be muffled.

The message was from FBI Head of Operations, Chicago Division, Cameron Johnson, who Goodall knew reasonably well.

Sit tight Steve, perimeters are secured and there are two CPD cars under surveillance. Where are you exactly?

Goodall quietly texted back. *Third office on the right. We have arrested Hannah Martin and I'm sure that the front desk guards are down by this time. Awaiting further instructions.*

Take cover and defend your ground Steve. We'll get to you as soon as we can.

Reuben kept his eyes glued nervously on the door. Goodall moved very close to Hannah putting his gun to her head so that she could feel the coldness of the metal. She shivered.

"Just one move or one word from you and I will press this trigger. Nod if you understand."

She nodded.

"Good," whispered Goodall.

Three minutes of absolute silence were deafening to Reuben but he kept his vigil focus on the door. Each second dragged, the tension was suffocating, until the unmistakable creak of a door handle was heard. Imperceptibly the handle turned but then stopped as whoever was outside realized it was locked. Reuben involuntarily jumped as a muffled thud was heard outside the door. It could only be a bullet coming from a gun with a silencer. As the lock flew with a clatter from its moorings into the room, the door burst open.

Goodall had already hastily moved to the corner of the office so as to be a little shielded by the opening door. Beginning to hyperventilate, Reuben slid off his chair, ducked behind Hannah, and fell onto the floor.

A heavy set unshaven man filled the door frame. Surveying the room in a rapid sweep he fixed his eyes purposefully upon Hannah. Two dull thuds sounded, and a red bloom began to seep its way across her white shirt. Hannah slumped back in her chair and her mouth went slack. He had obviously found his mark.

Reuben was horrified and shaking all over. From his relatively protected position, he couldn't actually see anyone so he remained still. Goodall waited for the gunman to get into his line of sight before he blew his cover, blasting the silence with a clean kill shot. The gunman collapsed dead in the doorway. Suddenly a strong calm voice echoed into the office.

"I'm Captain Mark Hamilton of the Chicago Police Department. If you come out now with your hands up I promise you will be safe."

"Not a chance!" bellowed back Goodall. "I knew it would be you! Come and get us!"

The terrifying sounds of a semi-automatic resounded off the walls as bullets sprayed into the room at chest height. Amazingly, the dead Hannah was the only body hit. At the same moment, the sound of more automatic bursts were heard from down the hallway. Six FBI men wearing kevlar vests and earnestly toting their weapons came into view.

They swiftly and efficiently took control of the situation. Hamilton, wounded but displaying remarkable calm, laid down his guns and was immediately cuffed. Two agents then dragged him, wincing in pain, down the passageway, into an FBI wagon where he was driven from the scene.

Another voice echoed into the chaos.

"Steve! You ok?"

"We are fine Cameron. Thanks."

Goodall looked around the room and saw Reuben still crouching under his desk.

"You can get up now, the cavalry have arrived," said Goodall to a white-faced Reuben.

"I'm not sure I like this business, Boss."

"You did well Reuben. It's never easy especially when it's your first time. I felt the same way some years back too."

Cameron Johnson was a burly man with a reassuring manner. He and two of his FBI men made their way through the rubble of broken furniture and shattered computer screens. They checked the body of Hannah Martin and covered her face with a coat. Goodall threw his keys to one of the men.

"You better uncuff her."

"I'm so glad you are OK, Steve. We will be photographing

the office for the next hour or so. It would be good if you and your associate could write a full report as to what happened here."

"Sure Cameron. The two guards?"

"Dead."

"Come on Reuben I know a place where we can go."

Goodall and Reuben made their way slowly from the devastated office. As they walked down the hallway, Goodall did a quick body count and deduced that there must have been five assailants in all. Now only Hamilton was still alive. Covers were over three men in the foyer and another two in the passageway. The walls of the passageway were badly pock-marked by several bullet holes and blood splatter was sprayed dramatically along the walls. About twenty FBI men wandered in and out as Goodall walked, his arm slung protectively across Reuben's shoulder, to his office on the other side of the foyer.

It was barely nine AM as the two men sat down in Goodall's office to write the report. The attack had happened and was over so quickly but it felt, to Reuben, that a much longer time had elapsed. He was still shaking and wondered how long it would take to fully get over it, if he ever would.

Albert Domenicci suddenly popped into Reuben's head, and he remembered that he had been formulating an audacious theory on the man's activities. Although itching to tell Goodall, he decided to wait until the report was completed.

Goodall pulled out a small flask of cognac from his desk drawer along with two shot glasses and poured amber liquid into both of them.

"Get this into you. It will do you the world of good after what you have just gone through."

"I need something, that's for sure," said Reuben as he sculled it down in one gulp. Goodall watched with a tough grin on his face as if he'd seen it all before.

"Now, how will we put this regarding Hannah Martin, I wonder?" asked Goodall looking a little puzzled. "We can't say what really happened because it sounds so ridiculous."

"Her wanting a date with me also sounds a bit weird too."

"Yes, but you asked and she took the opportunity to see what else she could get out of you. Let's see if this version of the story has legs for the report"

Goodall began to enter his rough version of the story into his computer, reading out loud to Reuben as he went.

"I believe that my lecture and the fact I mentioned Domenicci's name to Hamilton started the process. Hannah Martin conned my associate Reuben Cohn into believing she was going to cooperate with The Department by suggesting he get me to witness her statement to that effect. Cohn had a premonition that all was not kosher and told me to be aware of a trap. I could not contact the CPD so texted the FBI and played along with the charade. By the time I made contact with the front desk guards it was already too late to save them. I cuffed Hannah Martin and she confessed her part in the plan to make our investigation results disappear, organise an attack on the morgue and kill Cohn and myself. Hannah Martin was shot by an unknown assailant. I managed to kill the gunman who had shot Hannah Martin and stalled Hamilton until The FBI came and cleaned up the rest. They took the injured Hamilton away."

Goodall paused for breath, looking pleased with his hopefully credible account. "What do you think?"

Reuben nodded. "Sounds accurate enough."

Goodall quickly opened a new document and resumed his typing. His statement was pretty much word for word what he'd said to Reuben. He also added that he felt Reuben Cohn deserved a commendation for his part in uncovering the relationship between Domenicci and the Chicago Police Department. He printed it out on a sheet of A4 paper and handed it to Reuben who read it through twice. He was quite chuffed to see his name portrayed in that manner. Both Reuben and Goodall signed and dated the report and left the office to meet up with the FBI men.

"Is there an official investigation into Albert Domenicci?" inquired Cameron Johnson.

"None that I know," smiled Goodall. "We just went fishing and, even though we can't prove anything as yet, he sure is top of our pending investigation list. Just can't work out what scam he's pulling."

Raising a finger tentatively, Reuben interrupted. "I have a theory, Boss."

"Ok let's hear it then." Goodall couldn't help himself in adding, "But just don't make it too long."

Reuben took a deep breath. "Here's what I've been thinking. It's all about the weight of the freight he's importing every month from Sicily. When I checked his IRS records it all looked genuine and feasible. Profit per year around one hundred thousand dollars is not, in my opinion, enough to warrant paying off a dozen cops and whoever else is on his payroll. He imports olive oil at a competitive rate to not arouse suspicion. I checked other importers and the only difference was the weight, thickness and dark colour of the bottles. His partners in this business own glassworks, both here and in Sicily, and do their own bottling. I believe that they are manufacturing a special glass bottle with a double layer for the purpose of transporting drugs and anything else they can stash between the glass layers before they put in the oil and seal them up. The two wholesalers empty the oil into similar bottles and distribute as per normal. The outer layer of the original bottles are then carefully broken, the contraband removed, and the remains melted down again for the new crop of bottles."

"Are you telling me you worked all this out just from the IRS records?" asked Cameron, looking impressed and a little skeptical at the same time.

"It is only a theory, and if we can keep it quiet for another ten days we can test it out."

"Steve, you have a born sniffing dog agent in this young man. Keep me informed."

"I will Cameron. We owe you plenty, my friend," said Goodall shaking Steve's hand firmly.

"All in a day's work. I must say I hope your theory bears some fruit. Reuben is it?"

"It's Reuben alright, and so do I sir," said Reuben shaking Cameron Johnson's outstretched hand. The only sensation Reuben felt indicated FBI business.

"You two are cleared to leave anytime you want to." Indicating with his thumb in the direction of Reuben's office he added, "My team are still working in that office building up a crime-scene image that I'm sure will match your report. Good work, both of you."

"Feel like a burger?" said Goodall to Reuben as Cameron decisively marched off.

Reuben looked incredulously at Goodall wondering how he could even think of eating anything, especially a burger, after seeing so many people killed. *Poor Hannah. What is going on in the world?* thought Reuben.

"Just a coffee, maybe."

"I know a place," said Goodall smiling warmly at Reuben. "I know you might be feeling a little ill from all of this but sometimes these things happen in our line of work."

"I don't have to like it though."

"No you don't. Carrying on and getting the job done is our main objective while cleaning up the bad guys and protecting the good guys. I need a coffee too. We need to discuss Domenicci's next shipment of olive oil."

Goodall's Porsche thundered into life. Before too long Reuben and Goodall were at *Henry's*, esconsed in a comfortable booth, away from prying eyes and ears.

In his usual manner, Reuben wasted no time blurting out the facts he knew. "The shipments turn up every five weeks like clockwork. The next one should be in ten days' time."

"Good work Reuben," said Goodall, trotting out his routine response.

Mumbling through a mouthful of burger, he added, "Sure you don't want one?"

"Coffee's fine, thanks. I am a bit off food at the moment."

"Did you think you were falling in love with Hannah

Martin?" asked Goodall in a fatherly manner.

"Something like that. I mean, I barely knew her, but I just know it felt wonderful being around her for an evening. Then to see her all shot up was horrible."

Tears formed in Reuben's eyes. It felt strange for him as he hadn't cried since he was very young. He certainly hadn't experienced any emotion on the scale of the past twenty-four hours. He lowered his head over the mug of coffee and let the steam mingle with his tears.

"What should we do about the Chicago Police Department?" Reuben asked quite pragmatically.

"Nothing for the moment. Let the FBI make that call and explanation. Not sure if we should stake out the customs area either. What do you think?"

"I think the best move would be to stake out one or both of the wholesalers and bypass the direct assault on Domenicci until we are sure what we have. Don't want to alert him to what we are doing. I agree we would be too visible going for the customs area."

"Now you're thinking like a detective!" beamed Goodall proudly over at Reuben.

Goodall dropped Reuben back near the morgue and drove off in a rush. Reuben went straight to his apartment. It had only been a few hours since he'd left his home, but everything looked different. Maybe it was the smell that any place gets when sunlight has been filtered out. Maybe it was the bleakness and solitariness he now felt when looking at the second kitchen chair that he knew would never be filled by anyone. Maybe it was a feeling of loneliness that he had never felt before that now was consuming him.

Maybe it was an extreme shadow of grief over what had just happened to the only female he had ever hoped to love being killed in front of him. Maybe it was a fear that all women were not to be trusted.

Whatever it was, Reuben decided that two things needed to change in his life. The first was to learn to drive and the second was to find another place to live in a better area of town. His time at the apartment opposite the morgue was over and he was now treading water until he resolved the situation.

Reuben's eye was drawn to the overflowing rubbish bin next to the sink area. One of the local newspapers was still visible amongst the teetering pile on top of the rubbish container. Reuben fished it out, turned to the classified ads section and began to rapidly scan for driving instructors. There were numerous adverts all basically saying the same thing but one in particular caught his attention. It was a picture of kindly-looking man assisting what could have been his son. This paternal scenario, which had rarely happened for Reuben, struck a chord that resonated throughout his entire being.

"Why wasn't my father like that?" he muttered to himself.

Without further thought, Reuben dialed the number.

"Family Driving School, can I help you?" came the female voice over the phone.

"I think it's time I learned to drive. When do you think I could begin the process?"

"You're in luck. We've just had a cancellation. There's a spot open in about an hour if you can make it here."

"Book me in. I have your address. My name is Reuben Cohn."

"Ok Reuben, see you then."

There was something in her voice that reminded Reuben of Hannah Martin and a shiver of sadness went right through him. As he had never taken any time off work in the five years he had been working for the DA, Reuben made up his mind that a week or two right now would do him the world of good.

The driving school was about two blocks from the morgue and not far from *Henry's* either so Reuben locked up his apartment and strode out down the street. The sun had just popped its head from a bank of heavy clouds and it felt good for Reuben to be outside sucking in the fresh air. He enjoyed it so much he wondered why he hadn't bothered with doing more of it before.

He was twenty minutes early for his first lesson and was directed to fill in the required forms while he waited. The young girl behind the desk, though sounding just a little like Hannah, looked nothing like her at all. This girl had dark eyes and long dark hair. Reuben suspected she had Middle Eastern blood in her but that didn't matter much to him. He was more intrigued by her exotic appearance and secretly wished he had a girlfriend just like her.

The thought of having a companion was completely new to Reuben but, after his morning experience, there was a nagging need to share his feelings with another human being.

The form was quite easy to fill out and Reuben was very sure that the address he gave would be obsolete as soon as he could find a better replacement. While handing the form back to the girl their hands touched. It was accidental and probably went unnoticed by the girl.

Reuben was gradually becoming less surprised and more comfortable with the fact that, when he made physical contact with other people, he could expect to receive information about them. He was still at a loss to figure out why this strange ability had only recently manifested itself within him. He suspected it had something to do with working with the brains, and more specifically, the recent occasion when he had courageously, or foolishly, applied the electrodes to his own head.

Through only a brief touch of the young girl's hand, Reuben again learned quite a lot. He discovered that she had broken up with her long-term boyfriend a week ago and was extremely lonely, not having any close friends with whom to share her grief. He also learned that deep down she was suffering from a feeling of anxiety and despair that she would never be good enough or pretty enough to attract another guy. Reuben had a fleeting wish that it could be him to ease her pain, especially after the traumatic experiences of his last twenty-four hours.

Raheem Komani, the driving instructor, was all teeth as he grinned at Reuben beckoning him to come outside.

"Come! You must be Reuben. This will be a lot of fun, I can assure you of that," he said, shaking Reuben's hand very strongly.

From the handshake, Reuben gleaned that Raheem was a Syrian immigrant who was lucky enough to have been granted a Green Card a year ago. He was around twenty-five, five foot three, dark eyes and long dark hair that settled on his shoulders. Reuben could not get a sense of anything else, surprisingly, other than it was joy for Raheem to be here in the United States and to have a steady job that would allow him to send a few dollars home to his family.

"You must learn everything in this book if you want to pass the tests to become a driver. It is not hard," he said, handing the booklet to Reuben. "And, most importantly, you must impress the examiners that you understand and follow the instructions too," he beamed.

"I'll do my best," said Reuben, smiling and enjoying the man's friendly enthusiastic manner.

It is so hard not to return a smile that is genuinely given by such a happy chap. Reuben didn't mind being distracted from the past twenty-four hours' events. A weight had temporarily been lifted from his mind as he concentrated on learning a few basics of the car he was about to drive. The empty practice track behind the office seemed perfect for Reuben as he was sure he was going to need all that space and more.

Raheem drove first and explained the functions of the clutch, brake and accelerator.

"Not much to it, really," chuckled Raheem.

Reuben strapped himself into the driver's seat and adjusted the seat to fit the length of his legs. Raheem had pointed to the rear-vision mirror and instinctively Reuben adjusted it too so that he could see enough of the back view to feel comfortable. Reuben had seen his father do this on several occasions after his mother had used the car, so he knew what was expected.

"Very good!" said Raheem looking impressed.

"Do you miss Syria?" Reuben asked casually.

The question took Raheem by surprise as he had no idea that Reuben or any of his clients knew where he was from. What surprised him most was that Reuben hadn't actually asked him where he was from, but assumed it correctly.

"Sometimes I do and sometimes I don't."

"It's hard for me to understand anyone having to leave their home. It must have been a tough decision."

"That decision wasn't tough at all. It was a case of survival and practicality. What was tough was leaving the university I loved and my family and friends. That was tough," said Raheem quietly, losing the smile. "You are the first person in the United States that has asked me that question."

"What were you studying?"

"Final year of law. A lot of good it will do me here!"

"Oh, I don't know. The future has a way of sorting itself out and you just never know. You learned how to think and reason things out. A very useful tool I'd say," said Reuben.

Back in the car, Raheem had a somber, thoughtful expression on his face as he went through the first lesson of driving. Reuben kangaroo-hopped around the track a few times and seemed to enjoy the miniscule patches where the car moved smoothly. The hour was soon over and the car was parked. The two men wandered back into the office chatting amiably.

"You did very well for a beginner. You will be driving yourself in no time, I can assure you."

"Thank you Raheem. I'll be back next Saturday, with you, if you're available," Reuben said hopefully.

"I'll be here," Raheem said emphatically and turned to

the girl on the desk. "Jasmine, book Reuben in for next Saturday at this time please."

"Certainly," she said.

"It was a good lesson," Raheem formally affirmed to Reuben as he walked away.

Reuben handed Jasmine his credit card to pay for the lesson.

"Thanks. What did you two talk about?"

"Life, I guess and the uncertainty that is thrown up at people and how they deal with it."

"No wonder he wasn't smiling," she said handing the credit card back to Reuben.

"Yeah, leaving your country must be rough. A bit like relationships that you have invested your whole being in and then suddenly they are over. Do you know what I mean?"

A look somewhere between troubled and puzzled briefly crossed Jasmine's face. "Unfortunately, yes."

At a momentary loss for what to say next, Reuben suddenly remembered a rare Saturday afternoon when he had not been working overtime, and had slumped on the sofa watching a melodramatic soapie that was overflowing with self-help one-liners.

"Try to see the positives behind the hurt. There is always someone out there in a similar boat and now you are in a position to find them," he awkwardly blurted out. "See you next Saturday."

"Yes, see you then," responded Jasmine, trying to cover her surprise.

Reuben strode out of the office with a renewed vigor. Jasmine watched him cross the road safely, thinking what an unusual fellow he was.

Before too long Reuben was back where he had been three hours earlier with Goodall. This time he perched on a stool at the long counter, watching Henry expertly flip a burger and at the same time organize the fillings for the bun. At the far end of the counter sat a scruffy man, idly cradling a steaming cup of coffee. Other than that, the diner was relatively empty, with a few random scattered couples and individuals enjoying their lunches.

Aware of Reuben's presence, Henry wiped his hands on his apron, and turned to him, shaking his hand. Henry's trademark smile was not as evident as it had been earlier in the day.

"Can't stay away, can you?"

"I guess not. Your special burger and a black coffee thanks."

"Coming up," said Henry about to turn back towards the grill.

Titling his head imperceptibly in the direction of the man at the end of the counter, Reuben took his chance.

"That guy who robbed you a couple of weeks ago – that's him, isn't it?" he asked, speaking barely loud enough for Henry to hear.

"How the hell did you know any of that?" exclaimed Henry now getting quite upset.

"The real question is whether you want to have him shake

you down again or have this nightmare stopped."

"He said if I said anything he would hurt my family."

"I know. That's the way these thugs work. It's your call but you didn't rat on him. We've been watching him for a while. I'm reporting it to my boss anyway. See if you can stall him with a burger."

"I don't know about this," whispered a nervous Henry.

Reuben took a booth seat where he could observe the thug and quickly sent a text to Goodall.

Boss, I'm at Henry's and he's about to get shaken down again by the same guy that did it to him a couple of weeks back. What do you want me to do? Reuben.

Goodall's response was immediate.

I'll call the police and get over there. You do nothing. Let's see if we can apprehend him in the act.

Ok. Got that.

Reuben noticed that Henry had refilled the thug's coffee mug and could just make out the conversation.

"Get me one of those burgers and put two hundred dollars on the plate when you serve it up. You understand?" said the man in a rough growling voice, opening his jacket. Reuben assumed it was to expose a weapon.

The thug was around six foot three tall with a swarthy complexion. He wore blue jeans and sneakers, and a jacket with a hood over his head, shading his eyes. There was nothing redeeming in the way he presented. There was no way that anyone would have wanted to refuse him anything.

"I understand," said Henry, looking straight at him coldly.

At that precise moment, the door to the diner opened.

Jasmine was purposefully headed towards the counter when Reuben saw her and hastily approached.

"Jasmine!"

"Yes? Oh, Reuben, it's you. What a surprise!" she responded.

"Come with me right now," Reuben almost pleaded.

"What's this all about?" asked Jasmine, a little taken aback.

"Please, it's very important."

Reuben grabbed her arm and ushered her to a booth where he could still observe the thug.

"There is a robbery going on right now. The police are coming and there could be some stray shots that I really don't want you to get hit by."

"Are you serious? How do you know all of this?" she asked, obviously not believing a word of it.

"I called the police and they will be here soon."

At that precise moment, two burly uniformed police officers walked into the diner. Jasmine gasped and moved closer to the window away from the men. Reuben moved protectively closer to her.

"Don't worry. I'm sitting here just in case a shot comes this way."

Jasmine looked into Reuben's eyes and said nothing. Fear was on her face and he could feel she was trembling.

"It's reminding me of the way it was in Lebanon," she whispered.

"I'll protect you." Reuben sounded more full of bravado than he actually felt.

Jasmine and Reuben sat immobile, their eyes glued on the unfolding scenario at the counter.

The taller of the two policemen unclipped his holster safety catch, drew his gun and approached the thug from behind. Alerted by the sound, the thug spun around and grabbed his own pistol from his jacket. Henry, without a moment's thought, grabbed the nearest frying pan, a very heavy cast-iron skillet.

A bullet exploded from the thug's gun, catching the metal trim of the edge of one of the booths. It then ricocheted around the diner. Terrified, Jasmine huddled closer to Reuben, clutching his arm as the bullet whizzed by, alarmingly close to them.

By this time the second policeman also had his weapon out, and the two officers fired simultaneously. At exactly the same time, Henry, getting caught up in the moment and summoning a bravery he never knew he had, raised the skillet and slammed it down on the thug's head. There was a cacophony of sounds, and the thug fell heavily to the floor. It was over, almost as soon as it had started.

Most of the other diners were so engrossed with their mobile phones, earplugs in and heads down, that they were slow to notice the ruckus.

The tall policemen was now talking to a very distressed, ashen-faced Henry who was still clutching the skillet, looking like a petrified statue.

"I killed him!" exclaimed Henry, his eyes wide with fear.

The policeman faced Henry square on, speaking coolly and firmly. "Henry, you didn't kill him. We did. No need for you to get more mixed up in this. Go clean that pan, ok?"

"Yeah, ok." Henry felt numb, meekly nodded and followed the order.

Jasmine slowly released her grip on Reuben's arm and stared wide-eyed at him.

"You knew this was going to happen, didn't you?"

"Not everything. The good guys won and you are ok is all I care about, if you must know," said Reuben softly.

Jasmine and Reuben sat in silence for several minutes, trying to calm themselves and absorb the horror of what they had just witnessed. Henry diligently scrubbed the skillet. One of the officers called in an ambulance, while the other went to his van and rustled up a white sheet to throw over the body.

Amazingly, Henry had snapped back into his normal mode of operation, which he always found to be a great comfort when disturbing things happened to him. He finished assembling the burger, and brought it over to Reuben. The tantalizing smell snapped Reuben out of his near-catatonic state.

"Thanks Henry. That was a bit close for comfort eh? That guy won't be bothering you anymore. You better make another for my friend too."

"Sure. I know you. You work across the road," said Henry to Jasmine.

"Henry, Jasmine. Jasmine, Henry," said Reuben.

"Reuben saved my life just now," muttered a tearful Jasmine, still too distressed for any semblance of normality.

"Saved mine too," said Henry with a wink to Reuben. Normality had obviously retuned to him, despite his trauma.

Reuben carefully sliced the burger in half, handing the plate to Jasmine while he placed his portion on a napkin. She took a delicate bite, a touch of colour returning to her face.

Reuben watched her eat for a little while.

"Is it Yasmin or Jasmine?" he ventured at last.

"It was Yasmin, but the fools at the Immigration Department wrote Jasmine and I felt that with a new beginning, a new name wouldn't hurt either. So there you have it."

"I like both names actually."

Reuben took a large bite of his burger and started his messy eating routine. Jasmine, in some disbelief, watched him.

Jasmine dropped her burger onto her plate in alarm as a figure suddenly slid into the booth opposite them. It was Steve Goodall. She looked a little distressed at his uninvited presence.

"He always eats this way, I'm afraid," said Goodall.

On hearing Goodall, Reuben stopped devouring the burger.

"Hi Boss."

"Quite a morning you're having, eh? Good work again Reuben, you are constantly amazing me."

"Aren't you supposed to be shopping with your wife?"

"You and I are not in her good books at the moment. We are having a dinner party tonight with some friends and if you and your lady friend are free it would be a pleasure to invite you both."

Never having been invited anywhere except to his parents' place for dinner, Reuben ignored the offer, and resorted to nervous introductions.

"Jasmine, this is my boss, Special Agent Steve Goodall."

"Just call me Steve. Are you free tonight?" he said to Jasmine.

Jasmine said nothing, feeling a little embarrassed.

"We've only just met today," offered Reuben.

"Oh, I see. Well, you look like a nice couple."

"I am free," said Jasmine. "Just one condition."

"And that is?" asked Goodall.

Jasmine looked directly at Reuben.

"You eat like a pig! I bet you don't even know what this food tastes like, the way you shovel it into your mouth. Show me you can eat slower and better or else I won't go."

Reuben looked a little shocked at her outburst and glanced over to Goodall who was smiling very broadly.

"You had that coming, pal."

Reuben picked up the burger and took a small bite, practising savoring the taste. Henry came over with some coffees and the second burger. Seeing Reuben eating that way he couldn't resist a wise crack.

"You don't like my burgers anymore?" he said laughing.

"Ok, ok. I get it. I'll try."

The awkward moment dissipated. Jasmine burst into laughter as did Goodall and Henry.

"That's settled then. I'll text you my address and see you two at seven. Ok?"

Reuben looked over at Jasmine with a pleading look in his eyes.

"That will be nice. Thank you," she said still looking at Reuben.

"Must be off. See you later."

Goodall was gone leaving Reuben and Jasmine alone eating their burgers and drinking their coffees. Reuben's phone buzzed and he glanced down at the message.

Nice girl. 669 S Pulaski Rd, Brighton Park. 7PM.

By now the place was humming with policemen, buzzing around taking photographs and interviewing those patrons who were closest to the bar. The body of the thug was wheeled out on a trolley. Henry was trying to act as if it was business as usual, even though no further food had been ordered. Patrons were either engaged in police interviews, or chatting amongst themselves, dissecting what had just taken place.

Jasmine finished her burger and delicately wiped her greasy hands with the paper napkin. A little color had returned to her face and Reuben thought she looked stunning.

"My father was in Lebanon during his military service," Reuben offered, out of the blue.

"Israeli Army?" exclaimed Jasmine with some shock.

"No, American Peace Keeping Forces with the UN."

"But you are Jewish aren't you?"

"Sort of. Certainly not a good practising Jew," he laughed nervously.

"I am Muslim. Does that bother you?"

"Not at all," said Reuben wondering why he hadn't

discovered that about her before. "Not a good one either if you're eating Henry's burgers," he chuckled.

"That's right."

"I can pick you up at six if you like?"

"You can't drive yet!"

"Taxi."

"I have a car so why don't I pick you up here at six?" she suggested.

"Sounds like a good plan, thanks."

Reuben felt somewhat strange to be with a woman in this way. He certainly was making an effort to slow down his eating and it didn't go unnoticed by Jasmine who cracked a wry smile.

Reuben knew she was still suffering from her previous affair and while his 48-hour obsession with Hannah was in no way to be compared with Jasmine's experience, he felt some bizarre sense of empathy and connection, in that they had both experienced a loss.

For Reuben, totally inexperienced in love, the intensity of the emotion that he'd felt for Hannah had been part of a sudden steep learning curve that had affected him deeply. Hannah Martin was dead. Nothing he could do to change it either. Jasmine was right there next to him. Because of him she was alive, and still capable of feeling young and pretty again. At this moment, she saw Reuben as her savior.

A reporter from one of the local papers poked his head into their booth.

"Did you two see anything of the robbery?"

"Afraid not. Sorry," lied Reuben.

Jasmine looked at her watch and got up.

"My lunch break is over and I must get back. We close at three on a Saturday. See you here later then?"

"You bet!"

In a flash she was gone. A crisp ten-dollar note was left on her plate. She had worked out, over time and experience, that a coffee and burger, her usual Saturday lunch, always came to $8.20 at *Henry's* and with the tax and appropriate tip she always paid for it with a ten-dollar note. It was a small gesture but impressed Reuben. He did likewise and winked at Henry as he left the diner. Henry looked as if he wanted to say something to Reuben but the police were still there and other customers needed their change.

Out in the street, sucking in the cold air, Reuben finally felt he was starting to come down from the ghastly experience he had just witnessed and remembered his promise to himself. Checking out the various storefronts, he was hopeful of finding a realtor.

Surprisingly there were two. The one that attracted Reuben the most had a large sign that simply read, "Good Value Rentals". Good, value and a rental were exactly the things that he had in mind, so in he strode.

Behind the desk, surrounded by a plethora of rental photographs on the wall, sat a young, well-dressed man in his late twenties. Very shiny suit and a semi-shaven face, he looked the part.

"Hi, can I help you?" he enquired, looking up at Reuben.

"Window shopping. Could you show me what your best

available apartment looks like and tell me the price so we can go from there?"

"No problem. How big a place are you considering?"

"Hmm, two bedroom I think," said Reuben.

"Take a seat." The young man gestured across the desk to a very comfortable chair that Reuben immediately thought he'd like to have. Both men extended their arms across the desk and shook hands.

"Felix Santana," said the young man, and Reuben countered with his name.

It was now strange for Reuben to not receive some snippet of personal information from the handshake but there was nothing forthcoming. Nothing he could glean at all, except from the body language and the style of speech.

Felix took out a large folder with glossy photos of apartments. He opened it and, pointing to the first picture, immediately launched into a graphic description of the property's award-winning features.

"Eighteenth floor, views to die for, awesome entertaining kitchen, Euro laundry, polished concrete floors – this baby's got it all!"

The best property on their books didn't speak to Reuben at all – too high up and entertainment and laundry were not high priorities for him. His disappointment was quite evident.

"Not to your taste?"

"I'm afraid not. Thanks anyway."

As Reuben got up to leave, Felix extracted a very different

photo from his desk drawer and handed it to him.

The plush rust-colored carpet immediately appealed to Reuben, and when Felix told him it was on the fourth floor, the appeal was greater.

"It's not on the market as yet," said Felix. "If you like I can call you when it is. Should only be a few days."

Felix handed a small notebook and pen to Reuben. "Just jot down your number if you don't mind. You are local aren't you?"

"Yeah, sure."

After leaving his details with Felix, Reuben slowly walked home with a satisfied smile on his face. He had made a start on a few things and it had already been a momentous day.

Police cars still hovered around the morgue and Reuben slipped into his apartment as quickly as he could. A welcome hot shower awaited him.

Reuben chose the better of his two suits. It was black with double-breasted buttons that always reminded him of the uniform that was worn by certain American soldiers in World War One. The circular donut-shaped buttons. gave them the nickname the Dough Boys.

He had owned the suit for about four years but had worn it on only one previous occasion, a funeral of an old aunt. There was no way he felt comfortable wearing it to work and the times he did wear a suit he always chose the dark navy blue one that his mother had bought for him about nine years ago. They both still fitted him just as comfortably as when he first got them.

It was dark when Reuben locked up his apartment and strolled in a leisurely manner to *Henry's*. For some reason he had the feeling that all the major excitement he was going to have that day, or for the rest of his life for that matter, had happened and he would be safe. The black kids were still out shooting hoops. He eyed them nonchalantly. They already knew he was a local but were still just a little unsure of who he actually was. This suited Reuben just fine.

At a quarter to six, Reuben stood outside *Henry's* as instructed. Henry saw him and waved for him to come inside but Reuben waved back and mouthed, "Waiting for a friend."

There were no customers, and no police either, so Henry left the safety of his counter to wait with Reuben.

"You did me a big favor today and from now on your burgers are free," said Henry patting him on the back.

"Wow! Thanks Henry. You were the one that whacked him with the pan," laughed Reuben.

"That felt good too. Do you think I killed him?"

"Hard to say really. A couple of bullets in his head probably helped though. He won't be troubling you again, that's for sure."

Henry contemplated his mixed feelings over the incident. On one hand he felt a bit alarmed that he may have killed the guy, and on the other he felt somewhat proud of what he had done. Recklessness and courage seem to walk hand in hand with little to divide them most times. Henry never saw himself in either of those two camps and had often wondered how he would react in certain circumstances. Now he knew. There is no going back from something that has been proven to be within you. It was the realization that people would probably view him very differently as a result of no more than five seconds of action. Not to mention how he would now see himself. What about the rest of his life? Surely he could never better what had happened six hours earlier. Maybe better was the wrong word?

At ten to six a shiny dark green Daihatsu pulled up and flashed its lights.

"That must be Jasmine. See you later Henry."

"Have fun," Henry yelled back as Reuben raced over to the car.

It was dark in the car when he got in and the sweet smell of a musk perfume attracted his attention. Jasmine was wearing a heavy woolen coat that was buttoned right up to her neck. She smiled at him.

"I like that you're early."

"I didn't want to be late," said Reuben nervously.

"You have the address?"

"669 South Pulaski Rd, Brighton Park."

"That's good. I sort of know where that is but I'll key it into my GPS just to be sure," she said.

"Good idea. I have no idea. I'm in your hands. You smell nice."

"Thanks." Jasmine looked pleased by the compliment.

The traffic was quite heavy and, at one point during the journey, a shower of rain fell.

Reuben, feeling a little awkward and unsure how to make idle conversation, sat in silence staring at the road and the occasional wisps of smoke from chimneys. He imagined families huddled together around an open fire eating fish and chips out of old newspapers. Not something he had ever experienced. Somewhere, deep in his psyche, he had a longing to have had that warmth to lean on. Some memory of what normal people did on cold blistery nights. But in his household the usual routine had been off to bed while his parents listened to the radio. He had often secretly wished he would be invited to join them in that ritual but he never was and his father had ruled the roost tyrannically.

As Jasmine turned the corner into Pulaski Road she broke the silence.

"669 must be very close."

With the GPS chatting in the background, Jasmine found a parking spot near a house that had some lights on.

"This could be it," she said almost triumphantly.

Reuben stared at the house trying to make out the number on the wall in the dark.

"Let's give it a go, shall we?" he said trying to fake a bravado.

Jasmine turned off the ignition and they got out of the car. There was a light drizzle of rain but it felt good and calming to Reuben. This was a first for him to be with a real date and to be at his boss's house for a social event. As they neared the porch, the number 669 became crystal clear. This was definitely the place.

The house was of an older style without a fence. The only thing standing by the street was a letterbox. Strangely, it made Reuben feel welcome, as if he'd been there before. He knew he hadn't. Looking across to the neighboring houses he noticed that hardly any of them had fences. It appeared that some lawns were joined. *How very neighborly,* he thought; *they probably take turns in mowing each other's lawns too, as well as keeping a vigil for unwelcome guests. There are probably eyes watching us now from across the street.*

Reuben and Jasmine took some refuge in the shelter by the front door. He pushed the buzzer and they waited.

A very elegant lady in her mid-thirties opened the front door. She had long brown hair, her pants suit emphasized long legs and she flashed them a welcoming smile.

"You must be Reuben. Please come inside. My name is Joanne."

"Thank you, my friend is Jasmine."

Jasmine smiled nervously at Joanne as they entered a warm passageway. Reuben could hear a fire crackling away in another room and there were smells of cooking wafting from the kitchen area. The house looked to be built around 1940 and had been very thoughtfully restored with an abundance of old timber and art-deco features. Reuben's thoughts drifted to how his boss had meticulously restored his Porsche and figured that everything in his life would need to have that level of perfection or close to it.

"Let me take your jackets, if you like."

"Thank you," said Jasmine as she unbuttoned her coat and handed it to Joanne.

"I'll be fine, thanks," said Reuben.

"Ok then let's go into the lounge by the fire."

As they meekly followed, Reuben was immediately impressed by the outfit that Jasmine had on. She wore a vibrant red dress with a contrasting pink silk jacket that suited her perfectly. Before they reached the lounge, Reuben whispered in her ear.

"That guy that hurt you must have been an idiot. You look beautiful."

"How did you know about him?" she asked cautiously.

"I know the look. I've been pained too."

Jasmine smiled nervously and tentatively slipped her hand into Reuben's. He sensed her joy at being acknowledged, complimented and understood as well as her fear of how she would be received by the type of people she was about to meet.

"They will like you. Don't worry."

"You read my mind," she said and eased up a little.

An open fire was burning vigorously in the far corner of the lounge area. There was no hint of smoke in the room and it was warm and cozy. The area was joined by the dining room which may have been separate rooms at one time.

Steve and a few of his guests were seated around the fire sipping on red wine and nibbling nuts and crackers. Steve looked up as Joanne ushered Reuben and Jasmine into the room.

"My friends let me introduce you to Reuben, one of our bright sparks in the office, and his girlfriend Jasmine."

Reuben glanced over to Jasmine and grinned broadly.

"Girlfriend sounds nice," he chuckled.

Reuben did a little finger waggle at the group who raised their glasses in acknowledgment. Glasses of red wine were thrust into their hands before they could protest. Reuben wasn't sure if Jasmine drank alcohol or not but when she took a sip he relaxed and clinked his glass with hers. The only drinking Reuben had ever done, apart from the morning nip in Steve's office, was ceremonial on Friday nights at his parents, when he bothered to show up. A sobering thought crossed his mind. Last night he drank with Hannah and she was now dead.

A man rose from the sofa. "Jack Walters and my wife Suzie."

"Pleased to meet you," said Reuben shaking his hand.

"Hi," said Jasmine to both of them.

Jack had the solid build typical of a footballer. He gave the impression that he was a tough son of a bitch if pushed the wrong way but a loyal friend to those he considered worthy. From the handshake, Reuben deduced that he was an FBI man and longtime friend of Steve. Suzie looked like the perfect Barbie doll.

The other couple appeared to be more civilian types. Their clothes were casual. The man was wearing immaculately pressed blue jeans, a cream linen shirt and high-end sneakers. His wife was smartly decked out in a flattering black skirt, teamed with a white blouse.

"Frank Marshall and this is my wife Ellen."

Frank's handshake was firm and from it Reuben immediately got the vibe that here was a guy who presented a quiet façade to the world. But underneath there was a lot going on. Extremely disturbing and violent images were at the forefront of this man's mind, scenes so disturbing that Reuben found it hard not to recoil in horror. Images of a young woman cowering in fear were strong, and even worse, it seemed Frank was contemplating something dramatic this very night. Reuben sensed that Frank was up to his elbows in some sort of nastiness, that was most likely murder.

Who was this guy? Why was he a friend to Steve? Reuben pondered.

Steve motioned to Reuben to join him in the kitchen.

"Excuse us Jasmine, I need a quick word with your man on work stuff and then he's all yours, I promise."

Jasmine smiled again at the implication of the nature of their relationship and watched as the other ladies eyed her from toe to head jealously. Youth always has that effect on middle-aged people when reminded of what it felt like to be that young again.

"Will you be alright? I won't be long," asked Reuben softly.

"I'll be fine. Thanks though."

Reuben almost rushed to be alone with his idol and mentor again. The kitchen was empty of people but various pots and pans were simmering away. The aroma was very enticing, carrying the promise of a wonderful meal.

"Jack is a friend of mine from the old days. Now with the FBI."

"I know," said Reuben smugly.

"A very good guy. The upshot of this morning is that we are going to lay all the attack on the as yet unknown gunman and paint the CPD men as heroes and victims. Any other way will affect our relationships, if you know what I mean. Just letting you know is all. Ok?"

"Sure Boss. Say, who is that Frank guy and how do you know him?"

"Went to school with him and we played on the same football team for a while. Lives a block away. Why?"

"What does he do for a living?" asked Reuben, purposely avoiding Steve's question.

"He runs a thermal burner with a contract to take the garbage from the Greater Chicago area and turn it all into electricity which is run into the grid. Real smart businessman. What are you getting from him?"

"I know you're not gonna like this Boss . . ."

"Come on, out with it Reuben!" urged Steve, totally unprepared for what he was going to hear.

"He's a killer and is planning another one tonight," said Reuben almost casually.

"You must be mistaken!" Steve burst out, feeling somewhat angry at Reuben. "Whatever else he is, he's no criminal. You can bet your house on that."

"Sorry Boss, but the vibe was unmistakable," said Reuben looking very seriously straight into Steve's eyes.

Steve looked dumbstruck and said nothing for what seemed like several minutes. Different emotions seemed to cross his face, until finally, with a deep sigh, he said, "Well, don't say anything more. I'll keep an eye on him. Ok?"

"Ok Boss."

Steve still looked skeptical. "I would know if there were any unsolved murders in this precinct. And anyway Frank has an unblemished record; he hasn't even got any traffic violations as far as I know."

Although he recognized his boss's distress, Reuben persisted. "You know that I'm usually right."

"It doesn't add up. I've known this guy forever."

Reuben felt there was nothing more he could add, and the last thing he wanted was to upset Steve, especially on this special occasion.

"Shouldn't leave Jasmine. Is that all Boss?"

"Yeah, I guess so." Goodall looked deeply troubled.

Reuben wandered back into the lounge and sat next to Jasmine. She was obviously not having a good time. The conversation was at least 10-15 years ahead of her age group and background, and not a solitary person had even spoken to her.

Joanne called everyone to come to the table and dinner was served. It was as tasty as it had smelled and Jasmine was secretly delighted to observe Reuben practising his newly-acquired table manners.

Reuben kept a peripheral eye on Frank, but noticed nothing of any significance. The dinner party was dominated by the sort of conversation often associated with thirty-somethings, and which was of little interest to the younger couple.

Reuben and Jasmine felt somewhat out of place, and were hanging out to be back in the car heading home.

As the last guests left Steve excused himself from the clear-up. He slipped into his office and dialed the local police station. It answered on the second ring.

"Sergeant Polanski here."

"Goodall here. DA's office. Sorry to bother you on a Saturday night, but I have a rather urgent question. I'm wondering if any missing person's reports had been filed lately or if any unsolved murders have occurred in the past few weeks in this area."

Goodall heard the sound of a computer keyboard.

Polanski's voice came back on the line. "Nothing I can see on our records. Something you know that we don't?"

"Just checking out a hunch. Thanks. Good night!"

Goodall then phoned Jack, hoping he and Suzie had arrived home by now. They only lived three blocks away.

Jack recognized his best friend's number immediately.

"Steve!! Missing me already? Did we leave something behind? Lovely evening, by the way. Your Joanne is one mighty fine cook."

"Jack, I need a discreet favour," said Goodall, ignoring the small talk.

"I reckon I owe you one or two. What is it?"

"Put a tail on Frank right now if you can. Or do it yourself. I've got nothing to go on but a tipoff. The word is that he's killed some people and is about to do so again tonight."

"Are you fucking with me?"

"Nope. This is for real. There have been no missing persons so my guess would be, if it's true, which I hope it's not, homeless people from out of town."

"If word gets out about this and it's not true, I'll be finished and so will you."

"I know."

"You still want me to do it?"

"I have to follow it up," Goodall insisted.

"Well just as a random thought, he's got that big burner going twenty-four seven. Be the perfect place to get rid of a body."

"That's right. You track him down and I'll check out the burner. Ok?"

"Alright. Keep your cell phone on and I'll let you know if I spot anything. I still can't believe it."

"Yeah, well. It came from a very reliable source who's never been wrong. That's the only reason I'm following up. Believe me."

Goodall hung up the phone and put on his jacket.

"Got to go to the office Jo. Sorry," he called out.

"Is it that Reuben again?" she called back.

"Not this time. Be back as soon as I can."

Frank Marshall had left Steve's in relatively high spirits. The evening had been more enjoyable than he'd expected, and he'd been happy to see that Steve and Joanne's home had been more clean and orderly than usual. He couldn't stand things to be disorderly, or dirty. Everything needed to be in its right spot for Frank to feel comfortable in his skin, and in his life.

He had big plans for the rest of the night. Arriving home, he put a call in to his waste removal plant and spoke to the night foreman, Pablo.

"Pablo, I'll be coming in within the next hour to do some paperwork and the next delivery is not until four. So why don't you take the night off and I'll make sure the burner keeps getting fed from the conveyor belts."

"Thanks Frank. Much appreciated."

"Enough garbage to see us through till four?"

"Plenty. I'll go in about twenty minutes. See you later."

"Perfect."

Suzie, overhearing the conversation called to Frank from the bathroom. "You're not going out again tonight are you?"

"Sorry, honey. You know how what I'm like. Can't get behind with the work. You look ready for bed anyway."

"It was a big night for me Jasmine, but I'm sorry I had to put you through it," said Reuben, feeling a little anxious and guilty on the drive home.

Disregarding his apology, she asked out of the blue, "What exactly is it you do in your work then?"

"I work for the DA's Department as an analyst," said Reuben, not wishing to divulge the exact nature of his analysis. "That's how I knew there was going to be trouble at *Henry's*."

"Do you like your job?"

Reuben pondered the question and took a minute to respond to it.

"Up until today it was everything I had wished for. Now, I'm pretty certain it's not where I want to be."

"Because of what happened at *Henry's*?"

"Not just that. I want a normal life that doesn't put people in harm's way. Especially you. When I saw you walk into the diner I was terrified that something might happen to you. It was unbearable. I'm so relieved that it worked out fine this time. What if it hadn't?" he nervously prattled on.

"What would you do then, hypothetically, if you left your work?"

"Resume my medical studies I guess."

"You were going to be a doctor?" she asked, a little shocked.

"Yes I was."

Feeling secretly impressed but not wishing to show it, Jasmine tuned the radio in to a station that played Middle Eastern music and let it transport her back to Lebanon.

They travelled in silence for the rest of the journey until they reached the morgue, where they parted with the formalities of goodnight and thanks. Reuben watched her safely drive off.

The black kids, still shooting hoops, stopped and stared at Reuben. He waved to them nonchalantly and they waved back, more from reflex than a conscious acknowledgment. They were all locals. It was sort of normal.

Once inside his apartment he stripped off and fell asleep dreaming sweet thoughts of Jasmine all night.

The weather wasn't exactly great for surveillance. The drizzle had resumed, and was intensifying. Jack parked his vehicle a little down the road where he could observe Frank's house. The lights were on inside so Jack took the opportunity to sneak over to his friend's car which was in the driveway. Now in full FBI mode, he planted an audio and GPS transmitter at the base of the driver's side door. Jack sprinted back to his car, like a shadow in the rain.

Just in time. Frank emerged from his house wearing a dark blue plastic rain coat that came down to his toes. He clambered into his car and drove off slowly. Jack waited until the car was fully out of sight before he started to track Frank's movements from the hidden GPS.

Phoning in to Steve, Jack gave his first report.

"Steve, I have a tracking device attached to Frank's car and he's on the move. Be careful. My guess is he's headed to the power plant."

"Good work. I'm nearly at the plant. I guess I'll wait in a side street until you give me the all clear. I don't want him noticing me on the road."

"Ok then. He just pulled into Main Street. Got to go."

The phone clicked off and Steve drove to a spot around the corner of the plant and parked well out of any line of sight. Jack turned on his car radio and switched into the frequency of the bug he had put on Frank's car. The audio speaker crackled annoyingly before Jack fine-tuned it. The signal was clear. All he could hear was Frank's regular breathing.

The GPS indicated that Frank had changed direction, turning away from the plant and then stopping at an outer suburban bus depot. Still keeping his distance, Jack listened as Frank turned on his radio. Beethoven's Fourth Symphony boomed out. Twenty long, confusing, minutes passed before the music was suddenly turned off and Jack heard Frank's voice. He was calling out to someone.

"What are you doing here?"

"I don't know. I've been waiting for a bus for the past hour," came a girl's shaky voice.

"There's no buses running this time of night," Frank called out to her.

"Oh shit! I can't stay here all night!"

"Get in. I'll drive you to where they are still operating."

"I don't know."

Frank's smooth cajoling voice rang out clearly. "I'm a police officer. You'll be safe with me."

Frank opened his passenger car door. Rain started to come in. A skinny girl with ripped jeans and dirty sneakers came reluctantly out of the shadows. Her lank hair flopped over her forehead as she kept her gaze on the ground. With her backpack dripping, she got inside.

Jack's GPS was a cutting-edge latest model, with a neat function enabling the user to record any surveillance audio through the car radio. Jack pressed the record button and continued listening. Frank's car had started moving again. It was headed in the direction of the plant.

Frank turned off the radio. He kept one hand on the wheel while the other fossicked in his raincoat jacket.

"Where you from?" he asked the girl.

"Columbus."

"Ohio?"

"That's right."

In a sudden well-rehearsed maneuver, his left hand still guiding the car, Frank pulled out a syringe from his pocket and jabbed her in the neck. It was so quick and slick that the girl appeared to have no idea of what was happening. She made not a single murmur of protest as her frail body slumped pitifully in the seat.

Jack realized that the conversation in Frank's car had ceased. He felt his adrenalin surge as Frank's voice came over the speaker, but it was not the Frank he was familiar with – the voice was aggressive and sinister.

"You are nothing but garbage! Garbage!" Frank said as he turned his radio back on.

Jack immediately phoned Steve. "Something's happened."

"Exactly what?"

"He picked up what sounded like a young girl from the old bus depot and she ain't talking anymore."

"You reckon he killed her?"

"Not sure. Probably drugged her. Heading your way. Stay alert!" warned Jack.

"Will do. You too!"

"I think I better call it in. What do you think?"

"Up to you, but I would wait until I knew for sure what was happening. Think about it, an hour ago it was nothing but a tipoff and we still don't have any hard evidence, do we?" Goodall was always about hard evidence.

"Well no. But it just sounds like your source knew what he was telling you. Who was he?"

"I can't reveal it. That's why we better not call it in yet - we have to prove it or drop it."

"Then we have to prove it one way or the other. I'll join you at the plant. Oh, put your phone on silent."

"Thanks Jack. Good point. I knew I could depend on you."

"If he's not looking for us we should go unnoticed. See you soon."

Both men clicked off their phones and turned them to silent mode. The vibration function would inform them of incoming calls. Still playing the waiting game, Steve sat silently staring at the rain splattering onto the windshield.

Jack followed the prompt of the GPS and listened intently for any sounds from the girl. He couldn't hear a thing. Whatever Frank had done to her must have been fast and effective.

Ten tedious minutes had elapsed before Goodall noticed Frank's station wagon pass the side street and head towards the factory plant which was surrounded by a wire mesh fence, giving Steve a clear view.

A minute later Jack's Ford, with just his parking lights on, pulled alongside Goodall's car and Jack beckoned Steve to join him.

"Not sure how we should handle this. Any suggestions?" asked Steve cautiously.

"His car is parked so there's no other way than to get a little wet and go down there on foot. That girl hasn't made a murmur. I reckon he's going to feed her into that burner sometime soon."

"This is a bloody mess! Can't call it in with just a hunch to go on!"

"Come on," said Jack as he checked his service pistol and slid out of the car onto the dark and wet sidewalk.

The rain was getting heavier, as the two friends, who now found themselves working as an improvised undercover team, crept up to the open gate that led to the plant. Making their way into the grounds, they could immediately see Frank's car. It was parked near the entry to the building that housed the thermal burner.

Outside that building a big LED sign flashed a warning of the hazards once anyone entered the building. Not only did the building house the thermal garbage burner, but also a conveyor belt that ran night and day, feeding the burner with any refuse that had been delivered to the plant.

Apart from the heavy rain, the only sound Jack and Steve could hear was the constant hum of the burner. Jack had been there some years back and found it once again a place where he sure wouldn't want to spend much time.

Frank was nowhere to be seen so Steve cautiously made his way to the parked car. The girl was still there slumped over in the front seat. From the gentle rise and fall of her chest he could see she was still alive. He figured he had a little time up his sleeve before he had to attend to her. He decided to wait and see what Frank was going to do, so he placed himself in a great vantage point where he could see the office, see where Jack was positioned, see the car and importantly, see the entrance to the burner.

Five minutes passed. It felt like five hours to Steve. Jack texted, *Be careful.*

"Yeah, sure," mumbled Steve.

I'm calling it in. Steve texted back to Jack.

OK.

Steve dialed the special number of the Chicago Police

Department he had on his mobile. It answered very quickly.

"CPD, how I can I assist?"

"Special Agent Steve Goodall of the District Attorney's Department."

"Yes sir."

"I need a van with four officers and an ambulance immediately. You have my location I presume?"

"Yes I do." Steve never ceased to marvel at the modern GPS phone technology, letting everyone know where the calls were coming from.

"I am with another agent, there is an injured girl involved and one assailant. We need urgent backup. I suggest using your sirens once you enter the premises. Will explain all once the girl is safe."

"Thanks for that. We are already on to it. I'll contact you again in an hour."

The line clicked off and Steve texted again. *The cavalry is on the way.*

After a couple of minutes of inactivity that seemed like an eternity, Frank's form suddenly loomed in the doorway of his office. Purposefully Frank strode into the yard and headed towards his car.

"Frank Marshall!" called out Jack.

"Who's there?"

"FBI. We do not want to open fire. Kneel down with your hands behind your head."

"Is that you Jack?" responded Frank, surprise in his voice.

"Do as I say now and don't make any attempt to go to

your car!" called back Jack.

"You're not going to shoot me!" Frank yelled at his friend. facetiously. "How the fuck did you even know?"

Before Jack could answer, he was stunned by Frank's nimble movement as he darted back into the area that housed the burner. Jack heard a heavy bolt slide into position.

Steve took the opportunity to race over to Frank's car. Climbing inside next to the drugged girl, he gently slapped her on the face a few times to get her to regain consciousness. She opened her eyes and looked blearily at him, confusion and fear in her eyes.

"Where am I?"

"My name is Special Agent Steve Goodall and you have been drugged by the owner of this vehicle. We have an ambulance coming. You are now safe."

"Oh my God!" the girl cried and started sobbing.

Steve phoned home. After a few moments Joanne answered.

"Better be good!" she growled into the phone.

"Listen Jo, I'm at a crime scene that is still unfolding. I need you to go over to Ellen's place and then drive her to the disposal plant. She knows the way. Very important. Frank has barricaded himself in there. Police are on their way. OK?"

"Of course. Frank! Oh my God! I'll put on some warm clothes and do it now. What about the kids?"

"I'm glad you're on the ball. I'll get a policewoman over to our place and Frank's as well."

"I'll leave the light on for her and a note."

"Good girl. See you soon."

Steve rang back the CPD and arranged for the policewomen to be sent. All the while his eyes were glued on the factory door. The girl started to doze again. Steve shook her gently and her eyes opened once more.

"Very important that you try to stay awake. I'm not sure what drug you were given but please try."

"I'll try," whimpered the girl.

The wail of a police siren became progressively louder and shortly a squad van screeched to a halt in the compound. Three police officers got out leaving one behind in the van. Goodal bipped the horn on the car and they hurried over. Clambering out, and squinting against the rain, Steve fossicked in his vest pocket.

"Special Agent Steve Goodall," he said as he flashed his ID. "Frank Marshall is holed up in the factory and this young girl has been a victim of some drugging and possible attempted homicide."

The badge of the tallest of the three officers read Lt Jan Wolinski. He was obviously used to taking charge. "Ok Steve, we can take it from here."

At that moment an ambulance careered into the compound, throwing up muddy water from the puddles.

"Thank God!" said Steve as he moved to the passenger door and helped the young girl out of the vehicle. The light rain kept the young girl awake long enough for two ambulance officers to lead her into their vehicle.

Relieved that the girl was safe and off his hands, Steve still felt a sickening anxiety forming in the pit of his stomach. Frank was in there and regardless of what he'd done was still his friend, and from the look of these heavily armed cops, something bad could well go down.

"This is the police!" shouted Wolinski through a megaphone. "Come out now with your hands up."

Jack came out of the shadows and showed his ID to the officers. Everyone stared at the factory door listening intently for any sound. The rain picked up and drummed eerily on the iron roof. That, and the incessant hum of the thermal burner, was all that could be heard.

Joanne's car, with Ellen shivering next to her in a nightie and pink woolen dressing gown, crept slowly into the compound and parked near the ambulance. Joanne got out.

"Steve!"

"Over here!"

Joanne raced over to where Steve was conversing with Wolinski and looking like a drowned rat. He hugged her.

"What's going on?" she asked nervously.

"A bloody mess! Frank has holed himself up in his factory."

"What has Frank got to do with all this activity?"

"He tried to kill a girl tonight," replied Steve very calmly.

"No! How did you find out? I bet it was your new best friend Reuben!"

"Jack is over there hoping to get him to give himself up, the girl is recovering in the ambulance. I thought that Ellen could talk to him. What do you think?"

"I'll ask her," said Joanne as she raced back to Ellen.

As Joanne and a very confused Ellen approached Steve, Jack also joined them. The distress and confusion on Ellen's face evoked a surge of sympathy in Steve. *What must the poor woman be feeling – after all, it was her husband!*

Wolinski again switched on the megaphone and handed to Ellen.

"See if you can talk some sense into him."

Mustering her self-control, Ellen put the megaphone to her mouth. "Frank! It's Ellen! I'm scared! Will you please come out so we can sort it all out and go home! Please!" Ellen then burst into tears.

Everyone's gaze was fixed upon the door to the burner. All was quiet; not a sound or a movement, only that infernal, incessant hum.

Heads turned as a pickup truck drove into the compound. A small, swarthy, dark-haired man got out. One of the other police officers went straight over to him.

"Who are you and what are you doing here?"

"Pablo Gonzales. I'm the factory foreman here. What's going on?"

"You work at this time of night?"

"We have a delivery at four but the boss let me go home for a few hours. Ask him."

"Do you have a key to the factory?"

"Sure. Here, take it," said Pablo handing his key ring to the officer.

"Thanks. Stand here by your vehicle."

Pablo obeyed without a word. He knew better than to mess with white police.

"I have a key!" shouted the officer, hoping Frank would hear as well. "We are coming in!"

Wolinski and two other police officers dashed over to the door of the factory. One of them put the key in the lock and as he opened the door all three readied their weapons.

The factory was unpleasantly warm and the stench of garbage pervaded the air. The large space was lit up with strong fluorescent ceiling lights that shone onto a conveyor belt. Like a giant treadmill, the belt chugged away slowly and steadily, carrying mounds of garbage, some compacted into cubes, some loosely strewn, but all heading inexorably to a gaping black hole.

Frank was nowhere to be seen.

Wolinski hastened back into the compound waving his arms and calling out.

"You! You're Pablo, yes? Come over here and explain what this thing is doing and how to turn the damn thing off!"

Pablo sprinted over through the rain and headed with Wolinski back to the conveyor belt.

"The belt is feeding the burner," Pablo explained. "It will take an hour or more to fire it up if I switch it off and we have a delivery soon."

"Turn it off!" bellowed Wolinski.

"Ok. Where's Frank?"

"Good question. Where is he? Any other ways out of here?"

"Oh my God!" Pablo had visibly paled, his eyes wide with horror while his mind raced.

"What?"

Pointing to the burner with a trembling finger Pablo said, "That's the only other way I know to get out of here."

"Just turn the damn thing off and we'll sort it out."

The foreman looked distraught, muttering to himself in Spanish and then addressing the police officer. "That's just not possible. He was a wonderful man. Why would he do something like that . . . "

Pablo turned the machinery off by pressing the red button on the wall. The conveyor belt creaked and groaned until it finally came to a halt. The noise of the fearsome burner stopped.

Everything went silent.

"There will be a delivery in a couple of hours. What am I going to do?" asked a pragmatic Pablo.

"You do nothing until I work this out," said Wolinski authoritatively. "Special Agent Goodall come over here!" he called out.

Steve and Jack bolted inside, frantically looking around for Frank.

"Are you absolutely sure that Frank Marshall was here in this factory," asked Wolinski in his most official voice. "He sure aint here now and there's no other way out."

"He was here alright," said Steve slowly. In a feeble attempt at black humour, and not believing his own words, Steve ventured, "Well, maybe he jumped into that burner or something?"

"Ok, how do we check the remains of that thing?" Wolinski asked Pablo.

"No remains sir. Everything is vaporized. Oh my God!"

Wolinski started to look annoyed. "I haven't even established Frank Marshall was actually here at all yet." He turned to Jack. "What do you say mister FBI?"

"He was here," Jack asserted strongly. "I saw him go in and bolt the door."

Steve chimed in. "What you guys gotta know is that Frank here was under some suspicion of murder. We have a girl in that ambulance as proof that he was trying to do the same to her."

"I had his car bugged," Jack added, "and the recording should verify what we're saying."

Wolinski threw up his hands. "Hold it, hold it, you guys. This is a helluva lot to take in. We gotta tape up the crime scene, if it is in fact one, and get you guys down to the station to make a statement."

Then, looking warily at Steve and Jack he queried, "Official investigation?"

"No. A tipoff," said Steve. "We were just following up but had to make a move to save this girl you see."

The men looked questioningly at each other as Ellen suddenly appeared.

"So where's Frank?" she asked.

"We don't exactly know at this time, ma'am. A couple of theories but the truth is we don't know," said Wolinski, in an attempt to muster some sympathy in his voice.

"Pablo?" said Ellen, turning to the still shaken foreman.

"Yes Mrs. M, I think it's pretty bad."

Wolinski remained firmly in charge. "I'll get some forensic guys to go over this place and you lot better come down to the station with me. Now."

"What about the deliveries?" stuttered Pablo.

"Fuck the deliveries! Sorry about that," Wolinski said to Ellen. "They will have to wait until this is a bit better understood."

The aggravated officer marched out into the rain, busied himself with a phone call to the station, while Steve helped Ellen over to Joanne's car. The poor woman now seemed in a state of near collapse.

Another officer escorted Pablo to the police van as Jack and Steve walked slowly back to their cars and drove off to the police station. The rain had eased, but that did nothing to ease their somber moods.

Three garbage trucks turned up right on the dot of four, only to be told by the police that it was not going to happen until forensics had cleared the site. That might mean a minimum of thirty-six hours before the site resumed operations. After some discussion with the policemen who were guarding the entrance, the trucks drove away.

The Chicago Police Department was in a brown brick building, with a lot of glass and nothing much else to brag about. The shabby interview room had chipped laminate tables and harsh overhead lighting. It seemed barely large enough for the group of five exhausted people, all in various states of shock and disbelief.

Pablo seemed like the only person who reckoned he knew what had happened to Frank. He sat, mortified, in a corner and refused to look at Ellen or respond to anything she said to him.

"So where's Frank? He doesn't answer his cell phone. What is going on Pablo?" asked a teary Ellen.

Pablo shrugged his shoulders and buried his head in his hands. Ellen looked over at Steve and Jack.

"Steve, do you know what's happening?"

"All I know is that Frank was under some suspicion of abducting young people off the streets and disposing of them."

"That's ridiculous!" she screamed out. "You all know Frank! He wouldn't hurt a fly!"

"There's a girl in the hospital that will tell a different story, I'm afraid. Frank drugged her, that's for certain, and I have a tape with Frank saying some pretty bad stuff," said Jack. "He's our friend, but this is way beyond what we could cover for him."

"Oh my God!" sobbed Ellen. She was immediately comforted by Joanne who stroked her hand.

A plain-clothed detective came into the room reading notes on a clipboard. He looked slightly disparagingly at the group of people assembled, water and muddy boots messing up what had been a relatively clean foyer.

"Anyone shed some light on all of this?"

"I phoned it in - Steve Goodall, DA's office."

Holding out his hand, the detective made a brusque introduction. "Ezra Washington. Come with me."

Steve followed Washington down the corridor into a nearby office and sat in the chair he was directed to.

"Well, what's the story here?" asked Washington, stifling a yawn.

Assembling his ragged thoughts, Steve launched into as accurate a summary of events as he could muster.

"One of my sources on the street gave me a tipoff that Frank was about to abduct and murder another homeless person. I phoned Jack, who's with the FBI. We went separately to check it out. Jack first bugged his car and then followed him to an old bus shelter where Frank picked up a girl, drugged her and drove her to the disposal plant. I was stationed a street away from the plant and Jack joined me, told me about the girl in the car and we went by foot to rescue her and talk to Frank. He caught sight of us and locked himself in the factory and that was the last we saw of . . ."

Grabbing a notepad, the detective put up his hand to stop Steve.

"Whoa there! That's a lot of info. Let me just sort a bit of this out."

So Steve filled him in on the ins and outs of who, what and where, as Washington made copious notes.

"I see. What is your opinion of where Frank is now?"

"I'd say he killed himself in that damn burner. Where else could he have got to?"

"That's what we are trying to piece together."

"If I could suggest a member of our DA Department, Mr. Reuben Cohn, he is one of the best analysts and detectives we have. He has been invaluable in other cases for us and I'm certain he'll be happy to assist at short notice."

"You two were involved in a shooting earlier weren't you?"

"That's right. He saved my life."

"I'll keep it in mind. You can go now."

"And my wife?"

"Yes. And take Marshall's wife with you as well. There is nothing we can say to her until the forensic guys have fully reported."

"Thanks."

Steve left the office, closed the door behind him and went straight to Joanne. He glanced over at Jack.

"Just tell them everything Jack. I truly appreciated you being there, my friend. We are out of here."

Jack and Pablo waited patiently until Washington emerged once more. He called Jack into his office first. Pablo wondered when he would get home.

Frank's victim was a very lucky young woman. Doctors at Chicago Hospital had ascertained that she had not suffered any grievous injuries other than emotional trauma. After running a blood test to discover the nature of the drug in her system, they deemed it safe to give her a sedative. She was now sleeping soundly. Her immediate drama was over.

Joanne drove an exhausted Ellen home in silence. After saying goodnight to the policewoman who had been stationed at the Marshall home, Joanne tucked Ellen into her bed and called Steve.

"I'm staying here tonight Honey. You understand."

"Of course. Try and get some sleep if you can. You might need it."

"I will. Goodnight."

Steve glanced at the bedroom clock. It was six am. Somewhat fatigued by the emotional stress of the night, he climbed into bed and drifted in and out of sleep. When the clock showed one-thirty, it took him a while to work out whether it was morning or afternoon. The dull light of the overcast sky settled that dilemma and he lay in bed listening to the rain on the roof, contemplating the events that had led to his friend's demise.

His thoughts went back to Reuben. Steve was a little confused as to how he really felt about the young man. There was no doubt that Reuben had been right. Was always right. It was a great attribute for a detective, but Steve couldn't help but wonder what else Reuben might know about him that he wasn't letting on.

It was Reuben's "gift" that had led directly to the death of Frank, with whom Steve had shared some great memories over a long period of time. Frank was gone, and both Steve and Reuben had been prime movers in that chain of events. Steve pondered as to how little anyone really knows and understands the motivations and hidden agendas of anyone else. Though no bodies had been found, it was pretty certain to Steve that Frank had led a dark double life. All the incriminating evidence had no doubt gone up in smoke. Thankfully Frank's final potential victim was safe.

Steve noticed that his phone was blinking, indicating a missed call or left message or both. Taking a closer look he saw that it was from Reuben. Probably the last person he wanted to talk to. He thought about it and then dialed Reuben back. The phone answered very quickly.

"Hi Boss. Firstly let me say how much last night meant to me and Jasmine. Lovely time."

"Thanks. Not for us though."

"Frank?"

"Jack and I followed him. You were right, I guess. He drugged a homeless girl and was about to dispose of the body into the burner when we showed up. I believe he killed himself. Nothing left. Police forensics going over the factory as we speak. That thermal burner totally obliterates anything and everything. He was one of my closest friends, you know."

"I'm truly sorry Boss. What else could I do?"

"Yeah. You are blessed and cursed I guess. I'm thinking there's something else on your mind."

"Got a minute?"

"Go ahead."

"I realized last night that I am really missing Med School and that I want to go back and finish before the credit for the first year runs out. If I could combine my work with The Department on special assignments, I feel I can handle both things and end up as a doctor like I always planned to become."

"Well that is some news! There's nothing stopping you resigning but if I'm hearing correctly, you see a longer future with us as a doctor. Is that right?"

"Exactly. There is something else too, while I'm at it."

"Ok, I'm listening."

"Raheem Komani is a Syrian refugee who is now working as a driving instructor. Mine actually. He's a good guy with no affiliations with anything sinister and I can vouch for that. Raheem was in his last year of law when he had to escape. Just a thought. What if The Department hires him, arranges for him to complete his degree, and makes good use of him? Plenty of Muslim refugees who are not quite kosher and he would be invaluable in that area."

"And he would agree to do it?"

"I reckon he would jump at the opportunity."

"Let me think on it and we can discuss it again during the week. Take the next few days off as your office is being reassembled. The CPD have finished with it and I've arranged for a carpenter and painter to tidy it all up. Your computer is ok but the screen needs replacing. Blood on the carpet needs cleaning too. Should all be done by Friday."

"Thanks. I need to do a few things as well."

"I'll be in touch but between you and me, becoming a doctor sounds a very good idea. Speak soon."

"Thanks Boss. I am sorry about Frank."

Both men clicked off their phones and pondered the future. Steve rang Joanne.

"Hi Jo."

"Haven't slept. Have you?"

"A couple of hours. Rough night eh?"

"Ellen is asleep now with enough drugs in her to knock out a rhino. I should have taken some too but she was so distraught that I sat up holding her hand."

"Good girl."

"Not sure what to do with Ellen actually. Any ideas?"

"She can stay here with us for a few days if you like. We can take turns in watching over her."

"You're a good man, Steve."

"Love you too."

Steve then rang Jack. Steve's name flashed up on Jack's mobile, but it was Suzy who answered.

"What did you guys get up to last night? Jack didn't get home till midday and he's still asleep."

"Hi Suzy. Sorry about that. There's very bad news I'm afraid. It looks like Frank killed himself last night and we were there. Jo is with Ellen and I'm sure she doesn't know all of that. Just that he's missing. We can't tell her, at this point. Maybe you could give Jo a call and be of some support, what do you think?"

There was a momentary silence on the line, as Suzy took in the enormity of what she had just been told.

"Sure Steve. Jack didn't say anything to me about it."

"That's why I did. I thought you should know. We are all friends and this is the time to be just that. Tell Jack I called."

Steve made himself a coffee and pondered what to do about Reuben. There was no way he wanted to part company from him but he was going to be a constant reminder that Frank had died indirectly because of him. Reuben was also a thorn in Steve's side, pricking his guilty conscience that he had still done nothing about Cynthia and the pregnancy. Jo would be devastated. Fortunately, he was sure Reuben wouldn't say anything to anyone.

"Shit!" he said to himself.

As Steve sipped his steaming coffee, his mind went into

automatic problem solving. It was what he did whenever a comment or suggestion was posed that could involve The Department. Having a Syrian lawyer that he could trust would definitely be an added string to his bow. Without even meeting Raheem he knew that if Reuben said he was alright, he was.

In his mind, Steve calculated that the two admissions to The University of Chicago would cost The Department just under a hundred thousand dollars as well as the salary for Raheem. It was doable. It actually felt good for Steve to be distracted from the events of the past thirty-six hours.

The University of Chicago had a high-ranking law school, in the top four in the country, while their med school, Pritzker School of Medicine, where Reuben had completed his first year, was quite lowly ranked. Steve knew one of the deans, Erik Maardsen, from his high school days. Steve was hopeful this connection would make it easier to get Reuben reinstated as well as Raheem enrolled. Especially if they were both working for the District Attorney's Office.

It was well into the evening when Jack phoned Steve who had no new insights into the Frank Marshall case. It seemed the plant had been given the all-clear by the police and was ready to resume operations. Pablo had taken the initiative of temporarily getting the business going again. He organized the garbage trucks to recommence their deliveries and an uneasy sense of normality returned.

Everyone, other than Ellen, had concluded that Frank was dead and gone. She was still in a state of shock and denial. Her world had instantly gone pear-shaped and she clung to the fact that Frank was just missing and would turn up somewhere.

There was no evidence to link Frank with anything other than administering a substance to a young woman with probable nefarious intentions towards her. Plenty of theories but nothing to substantiate any of them.

The CPD however, in the wake of this latest case, realized they had been a little remiss of late in concentrating on missing persons, and potential abductions. So they decided on a two-fold approach. First they followed up on a number of cold cases of certain missing persons from out of town. Then they printed up a series of broadsheets, displaying warnings targeted at young vulnerable people out alone on the streets late at night.

Chicago was not small but had yet to crack the three million mark. There was too much crime and unemployment. In recent years the population was actually going down. Still, it was big enough to attract all sorts of weirdoes and criminals. The drug trade was still expanding too and the sort of police corruption evidenced in the Hannah Martin/Mark Hamilton matter didn't help. Doing something more in the missing persons department could only make the CPD look better.

Reuben spent all of Monday morning cleaning and tidying. The amount of rubbish that had accumulated over five years of below standard cleaning was considerable. It was only a small apartment but in every nook and cranny Reuben found a new job to do. The shower area had calcium deposits and grime marks on the glass door and walls so Reuben did his best to make it somewhat presentable. There was no way it was ever going to be in pristine condition. In the back of Reuben's head was the bond he was hoping to get back when he finally moved into a better place.

Around twelve, Reuben switched on his computer to get the phone number for Veteran's Affairs. When he did, a flashing message from Vercingetorix caught his eye. This was very unusual.

Hello Charlemagne, I am the wife of Vercingetorix. Sorry to report that Ted died last week from a very long battle with cancer. One of his last wishes was for me to let you know how enjoyable you have made his past few years. I thank you too. Ted was in considerable pain for the most part and playing with you, when he did, helped take his mind off the illness. I wish you all the very best, sincerely and warmly, Betty.

Reuben stared at the screen for quite a while repeating *sincerely and warmly* to himself a few times. No one, in his entire life, had ever written to him on a personal basis. *Why would they*, he thought? No birthday cards or letters from friends. It felt strange and good at the same time. Reuben re-read every word and wondered what Betty was like and how she was feeling. He did not feel the need to acknowledge or respond to her note but he did feel a twang of sorrow that confused him a little. He didn't know whether it was the death of Vercingetorix as a person or the loss of his chess opponent. It may have even been a realization that some things don't last forever and time moves on regardless of one's wish for things to stay the same. It was just one more door that had closed.

Reuben dialed The Department of Veteran Affairs and it was soon answered by a very efficient but friendly feminine voice.

"How can I direct your call?"

"Mental health for a veteran."

"Putting you through."

Another efficient woman then answered the call.

"Mental Health. What is the name and serial number for the veteran concerned?"

"Jacob Cohn, 73456287A74."

"And you are?"

"Reuben Cohn, his son."

"Hold on, I'll bring up the records." A few moments of keyboard tapping passed, and the voice came back on the line. "Ah yes. It's just come up. Now, what's the problem?"

"I'm afraid that my dad has become a bit violent towards my mother and I'm hoping you can assist."

"That's no good. I see here our doctors had prescribed some medication over ten years ago. Not sure if he took it or followed up privately."

"I'd say he didn't on both counts. Now that he has retired from his work, I believe he has become bored and angry at the world. Taking it out on my mother. Don't you have a mobile service to drop in on him and do periodic assessments?"

"We do have that service but there is a huge demand and a long waiting list I'm afraid."

"Ok. Put him on the waiting list anyway. It's a start."

"Still at the same address?"

"Yep. The only time he'll move from there will be in a box."

Reuben could hear the keys of the computer clicking away again. A thought came to him.

"What about giving him a job on one of your publications,

like *Stars and Stripes*? He could solicit advertising for you on commission or something like that."

"It's not such a bad idea. You'd have to contact our publishing department. Let me get you their number."

"Much appreciated. It would take a load off my mind, I can tell you. It would make him feel useful and productive working for Uncle Sam again," prattled Reuben excitedly.

Having got the number, Reuben clicked off his mobile phone and opened the fridge. There was very little in there. He was at a loss as to how he should spend his time away from the morgue. He'd never done it before. He thought he'd try out Henry's offer, but not before he had rung the VA publisher and put in a suggestion about his dad. Although he was told to put it in an email, he felt chuffed with himself and headed out.

As he passed the morgue, Reuben noticed a flurry of tradespeople and security vans obstructing the entrance. *Missing my office already*, he thought as he strode on.

His mobile phone buzzed. It was a number he didn't recognize. He answered it anyway.

"Hello."

"Reuben Cohn?"

"Yes, that's me. Who are you?"

"Felix Santana from Good Value Rentals. I have that apartment for you to look at if you are free?"

"How is an hour from now?"

"That will work. See you then."

The phone clicked off as Reuben walked into *Henry's* and took a seat at the bar. Henry saw him and came over.

"Your usual?" he said with a glint in his eye and a warm smile on his face.

"That's what I had in mind. How you doing?"

"Thanks to you, very well.

Henry's seemed a lot busier than Reuben had ever seen it. Nothing like the notoriety of a police shoot-out to bring in the customers. All the booths were full and there was an excited vibe in the air.

Henry placed a steaming mug of coffee in front of Reuben, and laughingly said, "Business is good. Probably more than I'm used to."

"You'll manage somehow," joked Reuben. "By the way, do you know a guy called Felix Santana?"

"The slick rentals dude?"

"Yep."

"Been in a few times over the years, pretty harmless. You leasing with him?"

"Maybe."

Henry slipped behind his counter and Reuben looked around at the faces of all the customers. No one he knew. He thought back to the Saturday where he helped rid Henry of a dangerous criminal as well as endearing himself to the lovely Jasmine. How fortuitous was all of that and he thought he'd better drop in or phone her. He was like a teenager with a first crush and not really sure how to handle the next move. She was experienced and he wasn't.

Henry delivered the burger with a smile, expecting to see Reuben pounce onto it like a ravenous dog, only to be a little disappointed when he didn't. Smaller bites seemed to be the order of the day. Henry left him to it. There was no entertainment or humour in the new style Reuben had adopted.

When he had finished, Reuben put a ten-dollar note on the counter as he was a little unsure if Henry meant what he said the other day. Henry came and cleared the plate.

"No paying here for you, my friend. Your money's no good."

"Thanks Henry," said Reuben as he stuffed the note back in his shirt pocket. "Best burgers in town! I'll send you broke!"

Henry was grinning went he left to serve another customer and so Reuben slipped out of the restaurant. He had another twenty minutes to kill before meeting Felix so he went across the road and poked his head in at the driving school. Jasmine was alone with her head in the computer.

Her look when she finally noticed him said that she was genuinely happy to see him.

"Hi Reuben, didn't expect to see you here today."

"I was in the neighborhood and the truth is I wanted to see you."

"What you doing then?"

"Looking at an apartment in a quarter of an hour with ..."

"Don't tell me Felix?"

"You sprung me. He thinks he's found what I've been looking for. So I'm going to check it out. If you're free why not come too."

"Can't, I'm sorry. You watch yourself with him. One slippery character that guy."

"I'm getting that message from Henry too," laughed Reuben. "I'll be alright."

"It's best you make these decisions yourself but I'll gladly look it over once you've decided."

"Probably a good idea. Is Raheem around?"

"He'll be back in a half hour I'll tell him you asked after him."

"Please do. Ask him to give me a call when he finishes work, I want a quiet chat," said Reuben handing Jasmine a note from a small pad.

"Sure."

"You free for another date anytime this century?" ventured Reuben.

"Friday night could be alright. What did you have in mind?"

"Dinner somewhere quiet would be nice."

"Drop by here at six-thirty on Friday and we can find something together if you like."

"I do like. See you then," called out Reuben as he left the office feeling inwardly elated.

"Looking forward to it," she called back. "Good luck too."

Good Value Rentals was only a couple of shops along and it surprised Reuben that the street seemed so quiet after the bustle in *Henry's*. Even the weather wasn't too sure what it wanted to do. Threatening to explode but only shedding a tear or two on the pavement. It was cold but not too cold. Reuben's coat flapped open as he walked. He didn't like to be too enclosed in clothes like some people did. Whenever he saw a person looking snug and warm with their jackets buttoned or zipped right to their necks, he always wondered why they did it. Maybe, he surmised, it was just a trendy thing to do and that because he most certainly wasn't in that trendy set, it was always going to jar with him. He hadn't minded

Jasmine doing it on Saturday night though.

Upon opening the door to Good Value Rentals he noticed that Felix was looking as immaculate as before. Moussed hair that was not likely to move an inch even in a thunderstorm. There was that shiny suit again, white shirt with cufflinks and a flaming red tie. Crocodile tan shoes with jet black socks. Reuben knew that this look would never be his.

"Good afternoon sir," said Felix extending his hand. "Right on time. Very impressive."

"I try to be," said Reuben, still a little amazed that he didn't get any insight from Felix's handshake.

"Come with me and I'll chauffeur you to two places I think will suit."

"Two?"

"A new one just came up."

Felix escorted Reuben to a shiny new Mercedes parked out the back. Brilliant blue with silver trimmings. Even Reuben was impressed.

"Nice car."

"Thanks, only had it a week. What do you drive?"

"Nothing yet. Still learning," Reuben said with a smile.

The first apartment was literally around the corner. *Could easily have walked there*, thought Reuben, but then the effect of the new car would have been lost. The Mercedes drove as smooth as silk on the road and Felix appeared to be a very good driver. Looked like everything he did, he did perfectly.

Parking in the side street between two other cars seemed effortless to Felix while Reuben tried his best to take in all the nuances of the maneuver to be used when he got to that point in his own driving lessons.

It was a small block, only four apartments. Very plain exterior that, in some way, impressed Reuben as he felt it was less attractive to unwelcome visitors. Felix showed Reuben where the stairs were and where the elevator was. They took the elevator to the second top floor. Only people with a special key and code could make any use of this, and it was one of a few things that Reuben ticked as far as security issues went. Hardly any noise from the street or anywhere for that matter. The insulation and design had most certainly not been cheaply done. This smelled classy all over. When the door to the elevator opened, to Reuben's surprise, there was yet another door which Felix opened with a key to bring them directly into the apartment.

There was a slight musty smell in the air as if it hadn't been properly lived in for quite a while. Dust had accumulated on the floor and table. The place was still fully fitted out with elegant older style furniture that also appealed to Reuben. The large double glass window was the most prominent feature as it gave a very good view of the surrounding area, including the Cook County Morgue and Reuben's current apartment block. Reuben gazed out the window and tried to imagine doing exactly that if he lived there.

Upon touching the dining room table to see if it was solid timber or just veneer, Reuben got a weird sensation, unusual in that it came, this time, from an object, not a person. The table was solid alright but something had happened here not so long ago. Sitting down on one of the soft sofas, Reuben knew exactly the story: an old lady had died here of natural causes. She had just passed on peacefully.

"When was the old lady found?" asked Reuben.

"How in the hell would you have known that?" asked a very startled Felix.

"I work for the Cook County Morgue and the DA's Department," responded Reuben, avoiding answering the direct question.

"Oh, I see. About two months ago. Mrs. Willis didn't have any family and it has taken this long for the County to release the property for either sale or lease. I'm working on their behalf. The County hasn't decided yet what to do with the contents, so they could possibly come with the apartment if you'd like that."

"Hmm, sounds good. Lovely view alright."

Reuben moved from room to room and took careful note of every minor detail. He thought that if he moved in, there would be very little that he would need to do to make it feel his. All the fittings and even the bed were of such quality and condition that it would seem pointless to change them just for the sake of it. Of course the sheets and blankets would have to be replaced and maybe the walls repainted with a different colour. Reuben had always disliked brown as a colour anyway. He immediately thought of a creamy grey and wondered what Jasmine would think of that.

There were two bedrooms, standard toilet with a smallish bath and separate shower cubicle. Reuben was pleased to see there was no ceramic lip to step over, like in his place. The kitchen had a reasonable bench space that looked in pristine condition like it had never been used. Reuben assumed it was a very new renovation and the poor lady had died without even trying it. It felt perfect, but Reuben was determined to see the other place before committing himself.

"This apartment looks very good Felix, we are definitely on the right track. Shall we go to the other place now?"

"Why not."

Felix meticulously readjusted a chair or two, locked the intervening door, and then unlocked the elevator with his key and pushed the button with a big G on it. The glide to the ground floor was smooth and silent and it wasn't too long before Reuben was outside looking up at the building as if he had already made up his mind. Maybe he had.

Felix effortlessly drove three more blocks away and then turned into a swish cul-de-sac where the apartment, that was first shown to Reuben as a photo, miraculously appeared in front of them. Reuben was determined to keep an open mind and went through the paces.

This apartment block was extremely impressive from the outside and would have suited most yuppies, as it was very modern in both setting and style. A block of only four units with underground parking that led to individual lockup garages. Mirror lining in the elevators. The first floor had two apartments, while the other two floors only had one on each. Reuben and Felix rode the elevator up to the second floor.

Security cameras appeared to be everywhere and Reuben wondered if they were just for show or in fact real and sending images to a central monitoring station. Three keys for the door seemed a bit over the top, but the way crime was in this city, anything that made the thieves' task a little more challenging was definitely a good thing. Reuben knew, as did everybody else, that no security system, no matter how elaborate, would deter or keep out unwanted guests. In fact, the more elaborate it was usually meant that the residents had more to hide.

The first thing that struck Reuben on entering this apartment was the thick plush cream-colored carpet. It felt so soft under foot and Reuben could imagine walking on it bare-footed. Nothing like his old place or Mrs. Willis's. Glass-topped table and designer furniture in the lounge area and quite startling black sheets on the king bed. Very small kitchen area but with granite benchtops. Reuben assumed that people who lived here would probably be busy workaholics who would normally eat out at fancy restaurants most nights or get takeout.

If he had seen it first, it may have had a stronger influence on him but the closeness to the morgue and Jasmine pushed him over the line with the deceased estate.

Felix correctly guessed that would be Reuben's choice. Felix knew his stuff alright. Now it was as simple as reeling in the line and getting Reuben to put his signature on the contract. Reuben, however, was toying with another thought. He figured he could possibly get a great deal to purchase it outright from the government authority handling the estate, especially if Steve Goodall took it on for him.

"Put a hold on it for me Felix. I need to run it by a few people first before I finally commit."

"No problems sir. Will three days be enough?"

"Plenty. Thanks."

Felix dropped Reuben back at the rental office and they went their separate ways. As Reuben marched towards his dump of a residence, as he now perceived it, his phone buzzed. Instinct told him it would be Raheem. It was.

"Hello Reuben? It's Raheem. You left a message for me?" asked Raheem somewhat nervously.

"Hi Raheem. Yes I did. I was wondering if you were free to have a coffee with me to discuss an idea I have."

"What is it about?"

"Nothing sinister I can assure you. When are you free? We can meet at *Henry's* if that is OK with you?"

"I'm actually free now."

"Perfect. Why don't I see you in fifteen minutes?"

"Alright then."

Reuben could sense a level of fear in Raheem's voice and decided not to add to it by furthering the conversation. Abruptly turning around, Reuben headed back the same way he had just come, and was soon in *Henry's* sitting in a vacant booth where he could see the door as he waited for Raheem.

Raheem spotted him instantly and made a beeline for the booth. Henry popped over as well. Reuben smiled inwardly at the sudden multi-cultural gathering.

When Reuben stood up to greet Raheem, the disparity of their heights became ever so apparent. Reuben towered over him and was also much taller than Henry.

"Henry, my friend Raheem."

Henry winked at Reuben and smiled at Raheem.

"What would you fellas like?"

"Just two coffees please," replied Reuben.

"No problem," said Henry as he made a swift exit.

"What's this all about Reuben?" Raheem still sounded nervous.

"It was something you shared with me the other day that I felt I could assist with."

"And that was?"

"Your sudden departure from Syria and your unfinished studies regarding your law degree."

"Oh that," said a somewhat relieved Raheem. "I've tried to move on from the disappointment of all of that. Nothing I can do about what happened to me and nothing really that I can do to get it back on track. With money I'm sending home, I can't afford any more studies."

"That's precisely what I thought, so I suggested a plan to my employers that could see you resuming your studies here at Chicago University while being employed where I work, the DA's office."

Raheem's jaw dropped. "Are you serious?"

"Well, it's only an idea and when I ran it past my boss he suggested I make absolutely sure you are alright with this concept before we take it any further."

"You would do this for me? Why? You've only just met me!"

Henry placed the mugs on the table, poured their coffees, indicating creamer and sugar in the bowl, and left. He was always savvy when he realized not to interrupt.

Reuben looked Raheem straight in the eye and attempted to reassure him of his sincerity.

"Let's just say that I know people, and you appear to me to be the sort of person who would appreciate the effort and be loyal to The Department should this all come off."

Raheem was still grappling with the enormity of what was being offered and the implications it might force on him regarding divided agendas in the future.

"If I agree, what would you expect of me?"

"To work with the company for ten years minimum when you have finished your degree, and to do the odd project regarding Middle East immigration issues to justify employing you while you study."

"I see. You feel I could be an asset in this area now that more of my countrymen are fleeing here?"

"Pretty much that's exactly what I thought. Proving your loyalty to The United States, fulfilling your passion to complete your law degree and being repaid handsomely for it."

Reuben let the words of his suggestion sink in as both men turned their attention to their coffees.

After what seemed a long silence, Reuben feared that Raheem might well decline the offer. But, ever the deep thinker, Raheem finally responded in a measured manner.

"Of course I would dearly love to complete my degree and the thought of being of some assistance in these times is also appealing. My warmest thanks to you for thinking of me in that way too. It has been such a long time when even I didn't think of myself as having a future where I actually made life better for people, other than teaching them the basics of driving a car."

Reuben noticed tears welling in Raheem's eyes.

"I am going to assume that you are for it then," Reuben said with a grin, trying to ease the tension a little.

"Yes, I am for it."

"Good. I'll start the ball rolling and see where this odd sort of process leaves us. My boss is also trying to get me in to Chicago University to complete my medical studies, so the best scenario is that we will be students together."

"And the worst?"

"That we have lost nothing by trying. I am thinking very positively about it all and will let my boss know of your decision. We will take one small step at a time."

Captain Mark Hamilton opened his eyes slowly to see Steve Goodall peering over him in the hospital ward. Hamilton was in full recovery after the surgeons removed four bullets from his abdomen. Realization flooded through the tough police officer that he was not in any position to resist anything. He had mentally resigned himself to spending the rest of his life in prison, to losing his family and possibly to being taken out by Domenicci and his cohorts. He was determined to play tough anyway.

"Come to gloat?"

"Nope. How the fuck did a relatively simple hit job leave the two targets, plus you, alive? That's what your mate Domenicci will be thinking. You probably took out the security cameras and that big guy took out the guards and Hannah," said Goodall surprisingly calmly.

"Pretty much."

"Why Hannah? And who was that big guy?"

"It was out of my hands. She wasn't supposed to be hit but I couldn't stop it."

"Who was he?"

"Mario Palucci out of New York. What's going to happen to me? Do you know?"

"If it was up to me I'd have you shot in some alley. Alberto will probably do that for me. The official story will see you as the only hero of the incident and now retired permanently from the force," smiled Goodall in a most sinister way.

"It makes some sort of sense I guess. It was nothing personal you understand. Couldn't control anything. Domenicci made all the calls, and now I'm pretty much fucked whatever way I turn. I guess it's my own fault. Short-term dollars with no exit plan except for a box or cement in a river."

"South America I'd say and pretty quick too."

Both men shared a look of understanding. Goodall certainly had his own personal problems but at least there was not a contract on his head and he still had a job to go to.

Reuben was desperate to get a smile happening on Raheem's face so he made a silly comment about Henry's recent antics with his favorite steel skillet. Raheem's big glossy white teeth gleamed as Reuben jokingly warned Raheem not to criticize the burgers or the coffees here. They parted with a handshake. Reuben at once gained an insight as to how appreciative and how surprised Raheem still was that this tall Jewish man, who was a bit of an enigma, was attempting all this for him.

"See you Saturday" was how they farewelled each other as Raheem paid for the coffees. Reuben continued back to his apartment. The heavens spat a few times but the real downpour only happened when Reuben was safely back in his rabbit hole. And that was exactly what he thought of it now.

Logging into the DA's website, Reuben soon navigated his way to the area that handled deceased estates. It was there alright. Mrs. Willis's affairs were being handled by a Sam Watkins, who was not known to Reuben. Sam's job was to manage the estate, and others, until they were sold off, as was the usual practice in cases where there was no will and no family that could be found.

Reuben wrote a note into the memo section on his phone to mention all of this to Goodall in the late afternoon after he had a nap to clear his mind a bit. Even the bed now felt like it had lost all of its springs and cushioning.

After resting for an hour on one shoulder and then the other he was quite sore and more determined than ever to begin the process of moving residence. A warm shower, for quite a long time, allowed Reuben to wallow a while as he let the water ease his muscle tightness.

"Hi Boss, got a minute?"

"Sure Reuben, how's your vacation going?"

"A few chores done but in general I'm a bit over it already. Do you know about my office as yet?"

"Friday morning I'd say. What's on your mind?"

"Raheem has agreed to come on board if you can swing it for us both."

"Very good. I've left a message for my school buddy and should hear back in a day or so."

"Do you know a fellow by the name of Sam Watkins?"

"Clerk in the city office I believe. What's he done?"

"Oh nothing like that," Reuben chuckled. "He is controlling a deceased estate that I had a look at today regarding leasing it and I thought that maybe I could buy it if the price was right and I could get a loan and do some salary sacrifice."

"I'll give him a call and suss it out. Text me the details. When do you need to know by?"

"Wednesday or Thursday should do it," said Reuben as he texted the address to his boss. "The fellow handling the leasing should get something for showing it to me, I guess, could you see to that as well? His name is Felix Santana."

"One thing at a time! Leave it to me. Anything else?"

"No, that's it, thanks. I'll be back to work on Friday. I don't think holidays are in my DNA. Be hearing from you then."

"You bet ya."

Reuben went back to his computer while Steve Goodall looked up the number and rang Sam Watkins. The phone answered straight away.

"Watkins!"

"Sam, I am Special Agent Steve Goodall, do you have a minute?"

"Yes sir. How can I assist you?"

"One of my top agents is interested in purchasing one of your deceased estates. Mrs. Willis. Do you know it?"

"Sure do. Just put it up for lease while we figure the best way to handle it for The Department."

"What would you say it is worth? Roughly."

"Around two hundred and fifty grand. Body corporate is about five grand a year too. They have an elevator you see that needs regular maintenance and they are not cheap toys I can tell you that for free."

"OK. What can you swing for my man? He just saved my life and I'd like to do something nice and legal. You understand?"

"I would say an even two hundred and waive all the sales tax would make it kosher enough for anybody, as it's staying in the family. Sort of," Sam chuckled.

"Thanks Sam. Put a hold on it for me and I'll get back to you."

"Will do, sir. Glad to be of some service to you guys in the field," Sam said with a sincerity that was overpowering.

Goodall then dialed his old school pal, Erik Maardsen.

"Erik? Steve Goodall."

"Steve, long time. How are things going?"

"I know. Busy as ever. I need a favor."

"Sure. DA business?"

"You bet."

"How can I help?"

"One of my top men, Reuben Cohn, needs to complete his medical degree and I have a Syrian refugee, Raheem Komani, who needs to complete his law degree. The Department will pick up the tab if it can be arranged."

"Cohn studied here?"

"Completed first year and then joined us five years ago. He is an invaluable agent. Raheem, I haven't met as yet but comes very highly recommended. Was into his final year before leaving Syria. They will both be working for The Department if all things work out."

There was silence on the phone, as Erik mulled over the proposition.

"I'll see what can be arranged. I know the members of the medical board and I'm one of the three members on the legal. An interview is a formality that must happen and I'll see if they both can fit into the next semester course starting in two weeks. The Syrian legal system and ours are very different but if he is a smart cookie and understands English very well it shouldn't pose too many problems."

"Thanks Erik, let's talk soon and catch up properly. Appreciate it."

"Sounds good, speak soon."

Goodall texted Reuben straight away.

The wheels are in motion. Arranged a very good deal on the unit for two hundred thousand dollars, walk-in price.

Body corp fees are five grand a year. Let me know if you want to proceed. The university boards have been contacted and they will get back to me re separate interviews for you and Raheem. Steve.

It was not until Tuesday morning that Reuben checked his phone and saw the message. His first thought was that Jasmine had not seen the place as yet. A second thought urged him to surprise her and make it totally his decision should the relationship not go as he would wish it to. His own assessment of the property was well over the price his boss had mentioned so he was pretty sure that he would buy it. With one hundred and thirty thousand dollars in his savings and a steady job with the government, he felt it would be no problem securing a loan for the difference. As far as the university went, he decided to wait before contacting Raheem just in case it didn't happen. He texted his response as he didn't want to have any confusions that might interfere with the purchase.

Thanks Boss, I'd say go ahead with the apartment and if you could give me some advice regarding a bank loan and salary sacrifice it would be even more appreciated. Speak soon re the university too. Many thanks again, Reuben.

Goodall phoned Sam Watkins to ask him to arrange all the paperwork on the apartment. Sam agreed to do it straight away. Goodall also requested that he make sure that the agent, Felix Santana, was duly rewarded with the same commission he would have received had he sold the apartment directly to Reuben.

It was around five when Goodall texted back to Reuben that a meeting with the medical faculty board had been arranged for him for Friday at eleven and that a meeting with the law faculty board had been arranged for Raheem for Thursday at twelve. Reuben texted back a thanks to his boss and dialed Raheem's number.

"Raheem, first hurdle is on Thursday at midday with the law faculty board. I will go with you if you like."

"I can't believe it." There was a pause on the line as Raheem composed himself again. "You are amazing. I cannot thank you enough. Come to the driving school at eleven and we will go together. Will that be enough time to get to the meeting?"

"I'd say so. A suit would be advisable, if you have one, and any papers from your previous uni would help too."

"I have a suit. Thanks again Reuben."

"See you Thursday then."

Reuben imagined that Raheem would be too emotional to continue the conversation so he hung up the phone. Talking is one thing. Getting the job done was another.

Outside, the rain pelted down on the old apartment block and Reuben could hear the sound of garbage cans being overturned by the fury of the wind. The only good thing about this building was that right now, with the storm out there, he was inside, relatively protected from the ravages of the real world a few meters away. He desperately wanted to remember other moments of endearment that he felt about his present home. The only thing that came to mind was when he moved in and escaped the tyranny of his father but he knew that didn't really count. The facts were that there weren't any other good memories. Full self-justification for moving on.

The black kids across the way and the odd stray cat would really be the only characters he felt he would miss. They would not miss him; that he knew in his heart of hearts. To the black kids he would always be the freak that frequented the morgue at all hours and appeared to have no life at all. Well, not the lives they were used to anyway.

Thursday morning, at five to eleven, suited up, Reuben poked his nose into the driving school office. Jasmine was busy typing away and looked up pleasantly surprised to see him standing there in the entrance gazing in her direction.

"Hi Reuben, going somewhere?"

"Raheem and I are going out for a bit. I'll tell you all about it tomorrow night if you like."

"I thought something was going on with him when he came to work in a business suit. He looks quite snappy too," she smiled, almost suggesting that he was now of some interest to her.

"Not too snappy, I hope," Reuben shot back with a twinkle in his eyes.

"Pretty good though."

Outside, the honk of a car horn indicated that Raheem was there waiting for him. Reuben smiled affectionately over to Jasmine as he headed back into the rain.

"See you tomorrow."

"Have fun," she called out after him.

It was still raining heavily, as Reuben scrambled quickly into the vehicle. He had no idea what kind of car it was other than that it was an automatic. Raheem did look very impressive in a navy blue pin stripe suit with double breasted buttons. It reminded Reuben of his father's best suit that he used to wear when he attended his synagogue for rare appearances on some of the High Holyday services. Jacob used to take his mother and Reuben too. Used to – but the last time in living memory would have to have been at least fifteen years before.

"I'm assuming you know the way," said a nervous Raheem.

"Sure do, keep heading for Lake Shore Drive, go a few more miles then I'll direct you to the parking area. How you doing?"

"Not very well to be honest. It's my one shot isn't it?"

"You'll be fine. Just be yourself and tell your story. The fact that you have been guaranteed employment with The DA's Office should carry a bit of weight. I've got my interview tomorrow so I guess I'll have to practise what I preach," laughed Reuben.

Raheem drove very well through the rain and in no time at all the university grounds were well in sight. On passing through the main gates, a guard on duty waved for Raheem to wind down his window, which he did instantly.

"Are you here for a meeting?" asked the guard amiably.

"Professor Erik Maardsen, Law Faculty," called out Reuben.

"OK, third building on the left. Parking across the road."

"Thanks," said Raheem and wound the window back up.

Big street signs were everywhere and the Law Building was easy to see. Old bricks and a well-worn pathway were all that Raheem could take in as they both rushed to the shelter of the imposing wooden doors of the entrance.

They had made good time and it was a bit of a relief for Raheem that the traffic had not caused him to be late on this auspicious occasion. He looked around the interior as if, in his memory, he was trying to compare it with what he had been used to in Syria. For some reason he couldn't remember any detail of his former school and a bead of sweat appeared on his brow.

Reuben noticed Raheem's nervousness and patted him on the shoulder.

"Once you get into the routine of everyday lectures, it all becomes very familiar, you know."

"I can't remember my uni at all. Isn't that a bit strange?"

"Nerves I guess," whispered Reuben. "This is the one that counts now anyway."

Raheem acknowledged that Reuben was probably right about that. A few deep breaths followed as a lanky middle-aged man also in a navy blue suit strode towards them with his hand stretched out.

"Raheem Komani, and?"

"Reuben Cohn, sir," said Reuben as he shook Erik Maardsen's hand.

"Erik Maardsen, pleased to meet you." He turned to Raheem who also shook his hand. "You must be Raheem Komani?"

"Yes sir, it is my honour."

"Good, your interview will begin in fifteen minutes time in Room 219; I'll see you there," he said and strode off.

From the handshake, Reuben had gleaned a small piece of information regarding a paper that Maardsen had written some two weeks earlier on the differences between law in the Middle Eastern countries as compared to law in The United States. Reuben quickly whispered in Raheem's ear.

"When you get the opportunity, mention that you have heard of the paper that Professor Maardsen has written on Middle Eastern law."

"But I haven't heard of this paper."

"Yes you have," said Reuben rather smugly, "you heard it from me right now."

"I don't know, Reuben."

"Try it."

Reuben sank down into one of the old-style leather armchairs in the foyer of the Law Faculty building, as Raheem made his way to Room 219. Raheem felt a bit like a condemned man going to his execution rather than a potential student gong to an assessment interview. Bravely he knocked on the door.

"Enter!"

Maardsen motioned to Raheem to take a chair.

"Raheem Komani, Professors Lewis and Matheson. Just a few questions as you come already highly recommended."

"An honour to meet you all."

"Your previous university was in Syria. Is that correct? Please tell us why you left without completing your course."

Remembering Reuben's suggestion Raheem looked each of the inquisitors directly in the eye and pretended he was in a courtroom situation. Taking a further deep breath he proceeded.

"Professor Maardsen I am aware of the article you recently published on Middle Eastern law."

"Really? You are well informed." Facing the other two professors he continued. "It was only six days ago in the Uni Gazette."

"I did not read it all but let me assure you all that our basic studies on human rights and the other aspects of civil law are quite similar in structure to the curriculum you have here in The United States. Of course there are many instances where we have a leaning to Sharia Law, unlike here. The premises are the same though. The real difficulties arise in the actual practice of what we have been taught. To navigate a course for a client without incurring the wrath of privileged people in our country can be quite hazardous for lawyers. Critical analysis of any sort towards these people can see a lawyer disbarred or imprisoned. Justice is a word on paper that is toyed with in examinations but rarely experienced by the average citizen.

"It was for this reason that I made a hasty retreat from Syria after being warned that a committee of judges wished to see me as a result of some student discussions. Most students who get called before such committees end up tortured and in prison. I decided that I didn't want to be in either situation."

Raheem finally paused for breath. The three professors then fired a series of legal questions at Raheem to see how he would handle them. They were very impressed by the way he addressed each question very clearly and to the point. At the end of forty minutes a unanimous decision on his acceptance had been reached. Maardsen faced Raheem.

"Your journey can continue here Mr Komani and I will send you a list of required books once you have filled in the application form at the front office. I understand that the District Attorney's Office will be picking up the tab for all your tuition and study. Thank you for attending today. We found it most illuminating, to say the least."

"Thank you all," said a very teary Raheem as he left the room.

As Reuben saw Raheem walk towards him, his phone buzzed a message and he quickly checked it out.

Hi Reuben, Doctor Deepak Gupta, head of medicine, will

have to cancel tomorrow's planned meeting with you but, after consultation with the other members and Steve Goodall, I see no reason why you shouldn't resume your studies again with us. Friday week at the bookshop to collect your curriculum requirements. Congrats, Deepak.

"How did it go?" Reuben asked Raheem.

"Wonderful, simply wonderful. I can't thank you enough my friend. You are the brother I left behind in Syria."

Raheem went directly to the front desk.

"An entrance application form please."

The lady handed him the papers without saying a word.

"Thank you," said Raheem. Still no response from the lady behind the counter.

Both men embraced and walked arm in arm from the building. The rain had now eased off to a light drizzle, but they were both oblivious to it.

Friday was a busy day for Reuben as he re-entered the Cook County Morgue. His old office had been given a complete makeover and the smell of fresh paint was not too strong but noticeable. Switching on the computers, Reuben meticulously checked that all his data and programs were still there. They were. The computers had not been changed, only the screens.

Two hours later a doctor in a white coat appeared and handed Reuben a cylinder. Extracting the severed limb, Reuben resumed his routine, almost as if it had never been interrupted.

By five, Reuben was already back in his apartment wallowing in a hot shower. Jasmine was on his mind and six-thirty could not come quickly enough. He dressed, taking more care than usual, and headed out to meet up with her.

"A surprise for you tonight, Reuben," she said as they touched hands affectionately.

Kissing had not yet been attempted and it seemed natural and easy for them both to take some time with that ritual.

"I sort of like surprises."

"I'm cooking for you at my place. I don't live too far from here. We can walk there if you like?"

"I don't mind at all."

Ten minutes later they were there. Jasmine's apartment, one of a big block of units, was about the same size as Reuben's. Single bedroom, small kitchen and an eating area. What she had done with it though was very creative. Strips of fabric hung loosely from the ceiling so that Reuben needed to either duck under them or, as he eventually resigned himself to do, walk through them. Jasmine smiled every time Reuben came near them as his facial expression showed a level of nervousness she hadn't picked up on before.

Reuben was nervous alright. Being in a young woman's home alone and invited was a definite first for him and he didn't want to break anything or come across like his old self. The dorkish days were gone, he hoped.

Tiny ornaments and reminders of her past littered every available space. Her family photo was what Reuben noticed first and identified her immediately.

"When was this taken?"

"Five years ago in Beirut. Both my parents are gone and my sister has married and is living in the family home. I left four years ago. Marina did not need me to remind her of what we had lost as well as the old saying we have, three's a crowd."

"We also have that saying," said Reuben.

"It seems that some wars simply don't want to end," she said sadly.

"I know what you mean. So you decided to give America a go and have a more peaceful life. How brave of you."

Jasmine nodded and it was clear to Reuben that she didn't want to continue the conversation. It was too painful for her. She ducked into the kitchen area and retrieved some plates that were warming in the oven. As she placed them on the table, Reuben could smell the cinnamon and cardamom aromas that were coming from the kitchen, and assumed, correctly, that what she was preparing for them to eat would involve those exotic spices.

Reuben unscrewed the cap of the wine bottle he had brought and let the liquid breathe, as he had seen Frank do just a week before. That memory flooded back with a vengeance and Reuben shivered when he recalled what had happened to Frank. He controlled himself so that she wouldn't notice. There was no way he wanted to spoil the evening. He wanted so much to get to know Jasmine better and let things take their natural course. The ifs and buts of any new possible relationship hung in the air enticingly.

Reuben poured two glasses of wine and instantly thought about Jasmine's Muslim upbringing and he softly called out to her.

"I've poured us a wine. Are you drinking tonight?"

"Thanks for asking, Reuben. I don't usually drink much alcohol but tonight I think it will go well with what I'm about to serve you."

"That's a relief. What is it?"

"Not telling. My mother's favorite."

"Smells wonderful."

Jasmine carried two dishes to the table. One was a lamb stew that looked as good as it smelled – deep rich brown, and so fragrant. The other dish was rice done in a very Middle Eastern style - onions, cardamoms and a few other spices that Reuben had no idea of. A drizzle of ghee on the rice and it was ready to be tucked into. Jasmine carefully placed the stew and the rice in such a way so as to resemble a circle within a circle and then sprinkled a few almond pieces over the meal. She looked very satisfied and proud of her work. They clinked glasses.

"Here's to you Jasmine and your mother's wonderful recipe."

Reuben made sure that he took his time over each morsel, making the right noises of appreciation every so often. The food was delicious. Reuben did not have to invent some outrageous comment as he knew that she knew he was enjoying it. She also knew he was making an effort to eat in a civilized manner too.

"I'm so glad you like it."

"You bet I do. Your mother would be proud of you."

"Ha! Sharing her dish with a Jewish man? I'm not so sure about that," she laughed warmly.

"I don't believe in religions anymore Jasmine. We are all the same. Just people."

"Yes, I think that too, more and more."

Reuben had two servings and felt that the evening could not have been better organized.

After helping to clear the table for some coffee and desert, they were unexpectedly interrupted by a loud banging on her door. A man's voice was heard outside, yelling angrily.

"I know you are in there with a man. I will kill you both!"

Reuben looked at Jasmine and she clutched onto Reuben's hand tightly.

"It's Pasquale. My ex." She simultaneously looked shocked, annoyed and worried.

"Let me handle it," said Reuben calmly.

"You better let me in before I break this bloody door down!"

Reuben released Jasmine's hold and opened the door.

Pasquale was a little over six feet tall with a tattoo of a dragon protruding from the sleeve of his shirt. He had a very fierce look on his face. He looked very surprised to see Reuben opening the door for him and even more surprised when Reuben spoke to him in a calm voice.

"You must be Pasquale. My name is Reuben, why don't you join us?"

"Who the fuck are you?"

"I told you. Reuben. Why don't you calm down and let's talk like civilized people first before you kill me?"

"Please Pasquale!" screamed Jasmine with tears forming in her eyes.

"One minute conversation man to man," said Reuben again and stared into Pasquale's eyes.

Strangely, after seeing Jasmine in such distress Pasquale softened just a little and stepped inside. Reuben extended his hand and Pasquale touched it with his knuckles. Reuben learnt a lot from that touch.

"Well?" Pasquale growled.

"You are not going to enjoy what I have to say, but it may save your life." Reuben let the words sink in. Pasquale said nothing but glared at Jasmine.

"You are a mechanic by day and a petty thief by night. I know this because one of your so-called mates has done a deal with the Chicago Police Department citing you as the main instigator in a heavy-duty crime. I personally don't believe him, but you certainly fit the profile alright. Since your mother died a year ago . . ."

"How the hell did you know that?" interrupted Pasquale.

". . . and your brother, who you love, is in the Marines, you feel angry and abandoned by the ones closest to you, don't you?"

"What do you know about anything?" Pasquale now had an a look in his eyes, betraying his fear.

"I know you and your friends are planning to rob Greeks Liquor Store on Mason Avenue this Sunday night. Ask yourself the question as to how I know that."

"Who are you?"

"A man throwing you a second chance if you have the courage to accept it."

"Pasquale, is this true what Reuben has said?" asked Jasmine tentatively.

"What if it is?"

"What if it is?" she yelled back at him. "Are you crazy?"

Reuben patted Pasquale on the shoulder gently.

"I work for the DA's Department and if you don't do what I am about to tell you, you will either be dead or doing serious prison time within a week. You understand?"

Pasquale looked wildly from Jasmine to Reuben, eyes widening as if he were going into shock.

Reuben pressed on. "Two things I'm asking you to do and I will try my best to get you off the prison sentence."

"What are they?"

"Apologize to Jasmine for the way you have treated her and promise never to trouble her again."

"And the second?"

"Be at my office on Monday morning at nine-thirty sharp prepared to write a full statement about your involvement with those other three thugs. If you like, I can get your brother flown in from wherever he is stationed to be with you, but it won't look too good on his record when it comes to any advancement, I can tell you that. He works for the same firm I do. The United States Government. You are a little out of your league in all of this, but it's entirely up to you."

"They will kill me," said Pasquale very softly. "Why are you doing this for me?"

"Well, if I'd known you were the one that hurt Jasmine so much I may have thought to just let you fry. But the truth is I believe there's a good man lurking in the shadows and I'm prepared to stay with that. If I ever get my driver's licence and then get a car you'd be the first person I'd consider to service it. From what I've learnt, you are a good mechanic. All of that would disappear once you go to prison you know."

Pasquale swallowed hard and took it all in. He faced Jasmine with the fierceness on his face now gone.

"Jasmine I am truly sorry for the way I treated you and if you could give me another chance,"

"No Pasquale. It's over between us, but I do accept your

apology. I've moved on and that's it I'm afraid."

"I don't blame you, really," said Pasquale, looking crestfallen and defeated as he turned to face Reuben. "She deserves better than me."

"Look Pasquale, I'd suggest that you go home and get that money you have in the biscuit tin …"

"How do you know all of this?"

"Don't use your credit card, if you have one, either. Drive across the state line and hole up in a motel until Monday morning when you will drive to my office. Of course you must turn off your mobile phone and keep it turned off until I tell you it's alright. Please try and stay out of any further trouble. You understand what I'm saying, don't you?"

"I understand. Too easy to trace me unless I pay cash for everything."

"Precisely."

Reuben patted Pasquale on the shoulder gently and it didn't seem to bother him at all this time.

"Oh, one more thing. Get rid of that gun too. If you do something silly with it then I'm afraid my task will be impossible. You won't be tempted to use it if you don't have it. See you Monday then."

Reuben scribbled the address of the morgue and handed it to Pasquale. He then opened the door. Pasquale took the hint, greatly relieved, but deeply shaken.

Jasmine stared at Reuben, her eyes wide in disbelief.

"What exactly is going on?" she demanded. "Did you befriend me to get to Pasquale?"

"Definitely not!"

"Well then?"

Reuben knew it was revelation time. If he wanted anything with Jasmine, he realized he'd better come clean. He drew a deep breath and nervously began.

"Ok, the truth is going to sound crazy. During the course of my work at the morgue I seem to have developed a special sense of what is in people's minds when I touch them. That is how I knew there was going to be a robbery at *Henry's* and that is how I knew you had recently been in a bad relationship that hurt you deeply. I only learned details about Pasquale tonight when I touched his knuckles at the door. I thought it would be for the best if I helped him rather than him pulling out his gun and killing us both."

Jasmine looked at him incredulously. "You've got to be kidding me! If this is for real, what am I thinking now?" she spat back at him.

Reuben took her outstretched hand and held it close to his chest. Jasmine could feel the pounding of his heart and she kept her gaze on his eyes.

"You are a little concerned for Pasquale. As for me, you are angry and confused, wondering what to believe, but at the same time you feel very close to me. You also wonder what to do next regarding us. You feel safe with me but feel that we come from different cultures and that the divide is too great to ever lead to anything permanent. You are missing the warmth of a relationship and not sure what to do about that either. Am I close?"

"My God! You know all that?"

"I am missing the warmth of a relationship too, not that I've ever had a real one. I believe we can make it work if you want it to as well."

The sincerity in Reuben's eyes was too intoxicating for Jasmine. She threw herself into his arms and kissed him full on the lips. Reuben surrendered to his much hoped-for first kiss. They hugged each other for a good five minutes. Jasmine's fingers delicately massaged Reuben's back and crept, ever so slowly, down so that he felt magic like nothing he had ever experienced before. He gently touched her body and learnt she was itching to be horizontal in her bed with him. There was no way he could resist. She unbuttoned his shirt and released his belt while he fumbled with her blouse. Body perfumes mingled with the musk fragrances of the apartment as they both removed all their remaining clothing. She led him by the hand into her bedroom where they both collapsed onto the bed with a thud that made them giggle.

"You've never done this before, have you?" she softly whispered to him.

"I'm so glad I waited for you," Reuben responded with his eyes wide open, gazing at her beautiful body. "I want you to be the first and last person too."

Even though Reuben was a little unsure as to what to do next, he had little difficulty in fulfilling the ritual he was born to perform. Jasmine caressed his head and back as he pulsated inside of her, both making the genuine noises of love and acceptance.

She had never felt that way about Pasquale and his rougher way with her. It was totally new for both of them. In each other's arms, and entangled, Reuben's eyes closed.

It was Jasmine's alarm clock that woke them. Right on seven o'clock. Reuben disengaged from her clutches and smiled as she turned the buzzer off.

"I must be at work at eight-thirty. Would you like some breakfast?" she asked

"Yes please. I'm surprisingly very hungry, even after what we ate last night. I love you Jasmine."

"I love you too," she said easily, and kissed him on the lips.

Reuben watched her naked body as she went into the bathroom and showered. He lay there wallowing in an afterglow that he wanted so desperately to last forever. He could scarcely believe what had happened last night.

"I've left a towel for you if you'd like a shower too," she called out.

"Thanks."

Reuben rolled out of bed and the coldness of the floor on his toes helped to fully wake him up. It was beyond unusual to shower in someone else's domain but it was the thrill of sharing and being accepted that filled his head as he toweled down and dressed again in his earlier attire. Jasmine had on a different outfit. Aqua blue skirt with a white blouse and turquoise neck scarf. She glowed with a radiance Reuben had never seen before.

When he finally glanced at his phone, there was a message from Steve.

Hi Reuben, just letting you know that the apartment is yours if you still want it and I've arranged a finance package that I'm sure you will approve. If you could ask Raheem to come by on Monday morning around ten we will start that process as well. Enjoy your weekend. Steve.

Thanks Boss, appreciate it and I'll let Raheem know as well. By the way, I believe there will be an attempt by four armed men to rob Greek's Liquor Store on Mason Avenue tomorrow night around 8:30. Maybe get a policeman to act behind the counter from 7:30 onwards. See you Monday.

Will do and well done Reuben.

Jasmine saw Reuben typing away on his phone as she laid out some eggs with cinnamon on two pieces of toast.

"Who was that?" she enquired, already assuming an almost wifely role.

"Steve. Great news about the apartment and also Raheem too. It might mean he will probably be too busy to continue at the driving school. I'll let him know when I see him later."

"That is wonderful news. When can I see the apartment?" she asked as she poured some coffee from a filter jug for both of them.

"Monday night if you like," Reuben said with a smile.

After breakfast, as Reuben walked with Jasmine to her place of work, she chatted about a dream she'd had during the night. It was such a joy to be able to share little things once again. Pasquale had not been a willing participant in such intimate casual chat, but she was sure that Reuben would be.

"I dreamt of my sister last night," she said pausing as she noticed a wry smile appear on Reuben's face. "Of course, you must have known that."

"I'm sorry that I have been blessed and cursed, but I'm so happy that you wanted to share it with me."

"I think you know more about me than even I do," she said trying not to frown a little. "My inner thoughts sometimes don't ever get through to me, but you get them, don't you?"

"I love you more because of them. Your anxieties are now woven into mine and I hope one day we can see your sister and her family. Maybe not in Lebanon but perhaps here."

"It's a nice thought alright."

They modestly kissed goodbye as they reached the driving

school entrance. Jasmine went inside and Reuben continued on to his old apartment. There was a lot to think about and the warmth and tenderness of love lingered at the fringes of both their minds. Reuben was also a little concerned that his gift might prove to be too overwhelming for Jasmine and he so wished it would not get in the way of their relationship. He knew that there was nothing he wouldn't do for her and he also knew that she was the sort of girl who would never do anything that wasn't what she saw as right.

On entering his old apartment, Reuben decided to start putting all the things he possessed into two distinct piles. One for taking wth him and one for dumping. It soon became crystal clear that the dumping pile was by far the largest. The table and the chairs had performed adequately but did not hold a candle to old Mrs. Willis's furniture. Even the five-year-old television set, as good as it was, was destined to be dumped.

Reuben thought about the black kids and wondered if they might be interested, so at twenty to eleven he carefully unplugged it and carried it over to the basketball court hoping they would be there. They weren't, but as he placed it gingerly right under one of the hoops, one of them wandered in, ball in hand.

"What you got there, my man?" asked the young man, who looked to be about nineteen and was the same size as Reuben.

"Oh hi," said Reuben in a way that suggested they had been long time acquaintances. "I thought, as I didn't need it anymore, that you and your friend might like to have it. It works perfectly well."

"You did, did you?"

"If you don't, it's ok. I can take it to a dumpster. Would you like it?"

"You can leave it here. You going from the block are you?" he said almost sorry that a familiar face was no longer going to be around.

"That's right. A bit further down the street. I have to run now, driving lesson, see you later then?"

"Ok," said the teenager, watching as Reuben strode off. "Thanks, my man," he called out and Reuben smiled and waved his hand into the air without turning around.

Reuben secretly wished that he had more knowledge and understanding of what the lives of these young men must be like. He knew, intrinsically, that the world they lived in had them starting from a position well under his. Below some of the migrants and refugees too. Human Rights had not, as yet, filtered to the masses. A lot of talk, banners and hand-waving seemed to cover the fact that not a great deal of progress in that area was being felt by the average African-American. Equality was a tempting word that offered much but mostly only delivered rain-drops from a storm.

Business appeared to be picking up at the Family Driving School as there was another eager learner, much younger than Reuben, filling out the form. Reuben had never seen anyone else in the office from the few times he had been there and it pleased him to see others using their services. This place was now special for him for many reasons. A permanent bond had been etched into Reuben's sub-conscious that pleased him a lot. Jasmine looked up at Reuben and he responded with a warmth that comes from familiarity and love. Raheem wandered in from the yard and made straight for Reuben.

"How are you, my brother?"

"Very well, and you?"

"Raring to go. Come, let's get started," he said with his broad grin exposing his teeth.

Reuben found that this lesson was very much easier than his first. After adjusting the rear and side mirrors, with much approval from Raheem, Reuben turned the ignition. After an initially jerky exit from the kerb, the kangaroo hops of the previous week were a thing of the past, as the car glided smoothly throughout the lesson. Even Reuben's parking was astonishing, given it was only his second lesson.

"Studying the booklet?" inquired Raheem professionally.

"I did look at it and it appears quite straight forward to me."

"Good. Believe it or not, I think you are ready to go for a test very soon. Not much more I can teach you," he beamed.

"By the way, Steve Goodall, your new boss, wants to see you on Monday morning at ten down at the morgue where we hang out. If you can get there at nine I'll help you with the paperwork."

"Wow! It's all happening then. I still can't believe it."

"You betcha. We'll be college mates as well, ha. It's going to be so cool getting back into the study routine. I'm really looking forward to it this time around."

"Me too. When do you want me to arrange your driving test for?"

"I'd say two weeks' time. I have a lot on," laughed Reuben.

"I'll get that started anyway and they will probably email you to confirm. I guess I'll have to hand in my notice here too."

"I'd say so. By the way, bring in your passport, driver's

licence and any other paperwork you feel might be relevant."

"Thanks, I was going to do that anyway. You never know what will be asked of me and I understand the process."

Reuben left Raheem pondering his future as he handed his credit card over to Jasmine.

"Tonight?"

"What did you have in mind?" she asked with a grin on her face.

"Six-thirty at your place and we can pick a restaurant together if you like?"

"You don't like my cooking?"

"You know I do. Just thought I'd like to take you out, if that's ok with you?"

"Six-thirty it is then. See you later."

People started milling around the counter and Reuben figured that a lunch break for her was not going to happen for quite a while. Business was business, and even though Jasmine only worked there and didn't own the school, she was totally committed to its wellbeing and would never lock up and go to lunch when there were potential clients already inside the door.

Henry's was as busy as ever. Reuben took the last available seat at the counter.

"You had a good week, my friend?" asked Henry genuinely as he poured Reuben a coffee.

"You could say that," replied Reuben. "You?"

"Look for yourself," Henry smiled. "It hasn't slowed since last Saturday. Your usual?"

"Yep. Thanks."

Reuben took the opportunity to text his boss.

Hey Boss, Raheem has confirmed he will be in on Monday morning. Have a great weekend, Reuben.

Henry placed a burger in front of Reuben and grinned when he noticed that Reuben was eating more slowly with smaller bites, totally savoring the taste. Reuben's phone buzzed with an incoming message.

Looking forward to meeting him. Brownie points from the CPD re tomorrow night's event. Fill you in on the details on Monday. Steve.

Reuben went back to his burger and coffee. There was a lot going on in his mind and in his world too. Top of the list was Jasmine and how special and important she was. Then there was the university and all that would entail, the new apartment and Pasquale. Not to mention what would happen on Tuesday when the new shipment, of whatever it was that Albert Domenicci was importing, hit the docks and got distributed. At the back of his mind was his mother and whether the Veteran Affairs had followed up on anything. He decided to wait and let things evolve and resolve themselves a bit more before he phoned her. She usually phoned him anyway.

Reuben smiled at Henry and mouthed, "Thank you," and Henry semi-waved in acknowledgement as Reuben left the diner.

When the light rain started to fall, Reuben felt like everything was fitting into some order in the universe and that he belonged. It was as if a certain stage in his life had finally ended and that he now knew for certain what it was that he really wanted from his existence and that it was achievable and within his immediate grasp.

The black kids smiled in his direction and he waved to them. It suddenly became clear to Reuben that most people live with a percentage of fear from things they don't truly understand or take the time to confront. His opinion of the black kids was his prime example. When he first rented the apartment, five years ago, his main aim was to get away from them and not attempt to enter their world. Now, that some familiarity and actual contact had occurred, their presence appeared normal. Even comforting.

Back inside his cave, the cleanup continued. The trusty stainless steel frypan with the caked on food grit beckoned to be dispatched and so it too went onto the pile of garbage. A few trips to the dumpster and there wasn't much left inside. Reuben's computer and screen, toiletries all stacked on the kitchen table, a pair of runners, the two suits, ten pairs of socks and undies, six shirts, two jackets, one of which was a plastic rain protector.

The bed, linen, refrigerator, cans of beans and spaghetti and even the kitchen table and chairs were never going to make the trip to the new place. Reuben had firmly decided that for the next two days, at least, they could stay as they were. Gentle reminders of what life used to be but was no longer. He figured that once he got the keys to move in to the new apartment, with or without Jasmine, not much evidence of his old life would be required or desired. This was of the ancient Reuben, and he was disappearing so quickly that, out of sight would ultimately mean out of mind, even for him.

Reuben fired up his PC and soon found the number of the agent who handled his present apartment. He dialed and waited for it to pick up.

"Rentals!"

"Hey, my name is Reuben Cohn and I'm planning to vacate my premises. Are you the right person to speak to?"

"Sure am, let me get your details from our files."

Reuben could hear the computer in the background as well as the tapping of keys.

"Ah yes, you been with us for just on five years, correct?"

"That's right."

"A long time for that property. You need help renting a new place?"

"No thanks. All sorted."

"Ah. When you planning to leave?"

"Next week if that's alright."

"No problem. I'll email you the form and all you need to do is email it back with the date you are vacating, drop the key back to us and once we do a check of the property I'll arrange whatever's left of the bond to get back to you."

"Ok, sounds pretty straight forward. Thanks."

The line clicked off and the buzz of an incoming email sounded. Reuben looked at the form and typed in all the dates as well as a forwarding address. He sent it back and it was done. One more task completed and ticked off.

A nice long hot shower with a short nap followed. Maybe, he thought, my last of both of these things here.

Leaving his apartment so as to arrive right on six-thirty, Reuben couldn't suppress his feelings of expectation and anticipation. He knocked on Jasmine's door. There she was in the sheerest of negligées looking like a goddess with more on her mind than food. Reuben was powerless as she literally dragged him inside and they both fell into each other's clutches. Clothes soon found themselves scattered on the journey to the bedroom as passion overtook them.

It was very different from the night before. The intensity was overwhelming for both of them. They slept solidly in a love embrace for an hour. Nothing like this emotion had ever been on the radar for Reuben and even Jasmine had never known the completeness of orgasm and afterglow that she was experiencing at that moment.

"I love you Reuben," she whispered in his ear.

"I love you too."

At just after eight o'clock that the pangs of hunger kicked in. They both appeared to be on the same page with just about everything. Jasmine ducked into a quick shower as Reuben re-robed. He watched her dress and it all felt so natural and right. Warm shivers raced through his body and he knew in his heart of hearts that she was the one.

Outside, the rain had picked up a bit but they managed to weave in and out of sheltered areas as they maneuvered their way to a little group of restaurants that Jasmine knew. Apart from *Henry's* and the company canteen, Reuben had little experience when it came to dining out, so he left it all up to Jasmine. She was pretty particular not to choose the expensive option even though it would not have mattered at all to Reuben. He was floating on a silver-lined cloud somewhere out there in the stratosphere, not wanting anything to disturb or drag him back into the real world. What was that anyway? The tectonic plates were not where they were a few days ago and would probably keep on moving forever now. If contentment was ever a word in Reuben's vocabulary, it now had a defined meaning. It was exactly where he was.

Reuben was totally oblivious of the restaurant but he did manage to maintain his new eating style. Slowly does it.

They ambled back to Jasmine's apartment looking like an old married couple, but once there it was all hormonal and the weekend disappeared in a flash.

Around seven in the evening of Sunday, two undercover police cars parked in an alley behind Greek's Liquor Store and one plain-clothed policeman wandered around the corner to the front of the store. He checked that there were no suspicious cars or people around and then ambled casually inside. Luckily, there were no customers at the time so he went straight to the counter where a balding man in his late fifties was poring over a local newspaper.

"Can I help you sir?"

"I'm a police officer," said the policeman showing his badge. "Are you Nick, the owner?"

"Yes, I am. What's the problem?"

"We believe there will be an attempt to rob your premises around eight-thirty, according to our source. If you could open the back door, some officers will come in and take up positions. I will man the front counter. Ok with you?"

"Is it the gang that I've been reading about, that's been terrorizing the neighborhood?"

"Could be. I don't really know, but I don't want you getting hurt when it happens."

"Alright then, where do you want me to go?"

"The back room for now and I'm going to set up some portable cameras aimed at the front door and road so we can monitor and record the event."

Nick quickly took his paper and unlocked the back door as three burly officers made their way inside. One of them had a small television monitor and quickly tuned it in to the two cameras that had just been positioned. On a split screen, a clear view of the front door and the parking area flashed up on the set. Nick and the officers' eyes were glued to the empty screen for quite a while.

Seeing a man wander in, the police officer became alert and looked over in Nick's direction. Nick's eyes lit up.

"That's Stavro, a regular of mine."

"No talking at all please," said the officer to Nick. He then spoke into a small microphone to the officer manning the front counter. "He's a friend of the owner. Nothing happening outside."

A well-dressed man in his late thirties, around six feet tall with a heavy black overcoat, came straight to the counter.

"Where's Nick?"

"Had to go someplace. He'll be back later. What can I do for you?"

"Plomari, thanks."

"What's that? I don't think I know that drink?"

"Ouzo!" Stavros said pointing to the top shelf. "The best ouzo too," he said putting a twenty-dollar note on the counter.

"Ok, thanks for the tip," said the officer as he got the bottle and handed it to the man.

"Thanks, tell Nick I came in. Stavros."

"I will."

Stavros exited the store just as a homeless would-be drunk wandered in and started looking at the shelves of alcohol.

"Any samples?" he laughed and then turned serious with pleading eyes. "I need a drink, bad."

"On your way buster. Nothing here for you. Beat it!"

"Nick used to give me a nip, where is he?"

At precisely that moment a black Ford station wagon with three hooded characters inside circled the store and then parked outside. Two suspicious looking men with long coats stepped out and headed towards the store entrance. The officer watching the screen in the back room immediately alerted the officer manning the front counter.

"Joe, I believe it's our guys. Watch yourself."

Joe turned to the would-be drunk and pointed to the back room.

"There's an open bottle of whisky on the table. Go help yourself and I'll join you too in a minute."

"Well thanks, I will," said the man and quickly tottered into the back room where he, along with Nick for his protection, were swiftly removed and taken away to one of the police cars out the back.

Two men, now wearing balaclavas under their hoodies, entered the front door. Joe pulled out his hand gun and positioned it so that they couldn't see it.

"Can I help you guys?"

"Empty the register and be quick about it," yelled one of the men as they both whipped AK47s. out from under their coats.

"Take it all! Don't shoot me, I'm no hero!" bluffed Joe. "There's a portable safe with the day's takings on the fridge in the back room. I'll get it for you, just don't shoot me please."

"You stay where you are, watch him," yelled the taller of the men to his side-kick. "I'll get the safe."

With one thief aiming his weapon at Joe, the other moved

towards the back room.

Outside, in the now pouring rain, two officers made their way to the parked car where the getaway driver sat nervously watching the front door of the liquor store. While one officer was tapping on the window pretending to want a light for a cigarette, the other slipped into the back seat of the car and coolly placed his revolver against the head of the driver.

"Get out real slow with your hands above your head. Any move other than that and we will shoot. Understand?"

"Yes sir," said the driver as he got out gingerly with his hands in the air.

Quickly cuffed, he was taken away.

Inside the store, one of the thieves opened the back room door and pointed his gun inside menacingly. The police, hiding there, were expecting him, and opened up with a barrage of their own. The sound of shattering glass was deafening, as the bullets smashed countless bottles. A heavy thud was heard, and when the police turned on the lights, they saw the invader had been killed instantly. In the confusion, Joe, behind the counter, pulled out his forty-four Magnum and shot the second thief in the chest and head before the guy could release a spray from his AK47.

It was all over in less than ninety seconds. Joe checked the gunman he had shot and found he was barely alive, so called for an ambulance on his mobile phone.

"Greek's Liquor Store on Dixon quickly, there's a man down, possibly two. I'm Senior Sergeant Joe Rocchi from CPD."

An officer came into view, escorting Nick through the rear room back into his store. There was a look of total disbelief on the shopkeeper's face as he surveyed the mess of broken bottles and the dead thief lying on the ground.

"Oh my God!" he exclaimed with shock.

"Lucky it wasn't you, I'd say," called out Joe who was still up the front applying some pressure to the surviving gunman's wounds.

In less than five minutes, the ambulance arrived along with a forensic team and two photographers. Nick was fascinated by the whole drama, but for the incoming team it was all a part of their regular routine. They seemed to display little emotion. They had seen it all before. Nothing new here. By the time the ambulance came, however, the wounded gunman had died and they carried his body away to the van on a stretcher. Very routine to all but Nick. Lost for words he just stared at the mess and contemplated what might have been the scenario if the police had not turned up.

Reuben and Jasmine slept together as soundly as kittens. They had found positions that made their bodies a perfect fit. When Reuben's mobile phone alarm went off at seven, even though he didn't really want to get up, he untangled himself and slid into a shower. Once finished, he put on his now well-worn undies, shirt, socks and trousers. He knew he couldn't go to work like that and that he would have to duck back into the old apartment to change.

He emerged from the bathroom to find Jasmine fully awake.

"Good morning," she said very dreamily.

"You know I don't want to leave you but it's a work day. It's been the best weekend of my life," said Reuben as he kissed her on the lips.

He was getting to be very good at kissing. There was nothing about Jasmine that he didn't simply adore and love. As he tied his shoelaces, she was putting a piece of toast into the little toaster and firing up the coffee machine. There she was in her dressing gown. He imagined the same scene as something they could be sharing in twenty years' time.

Reuben appeared to be drifting back into his old eating style as he hoed into the toast and coffee. He noticed her watching him.

"I don't want to be late today, sorry."

"Big day alright. Especially for Raheem. I bet he's excited too."

"Not to mention Pasquale. I'll see what I can do for him," said Reuben as he got up from the table.

"You're a good man, Reuben. See you tonight?"

"You bet. I'm hoping to have the keys to my new apartment too so we can go there together after work."

"Sounds good to me," she said kissing him at the doorway.

Reuben ran all the way to his old apartment, dressed in fresh clothing, and was in his office right on eight-thirty. The morgue did not yet have its routine hum of busy people rushing around. Reuben settled into his chair and switched on his computer. As it was going through the Windows initialization, Raheem knocked on his open door.

"Ah Raheem, good to see you bright and early," said Reuben shaking Raheem's hand warmly.

"This is one appointment I didn't want to be late for," he laughed, his big teeth glistening as he spoke.

"Steve Goodall, my boss, will be in at ten. But I want you to sit in on an interview with a guy, if he turns up, so that you can plan a defense for him later in the day."

"Already? You don't mess around. Who is it for?"

"Jasmine's ex-boyfriend, Pasquale. Do you know him?"

"I've seen him once or twice. Not a nice fella if you want my opinion. What has he done?"

"Petty thieving. He also has assisted The Department with news of a robbery that may have taken place last night. He's prepared to write a full summary of his activities over the past two months. I believe he is a troubled man over the death of his mother a year ago and wants to right the wrongs he has done as a sort of redemption."

"I see. You want me to speak to a judge on his behalf that he is truly remorseful for his past wayward behavior and that some repayment scheme and community service would be preferable to that of a jail sentence."

"That is exactly what I had in mind. Let's see if he turns up anyway."

Raheem took out a note pad from his briefcase and jotted down a few points. Reuben went back to his computer and started downloading emails. Most were usually junk mail with the odd item from his accountant or bank indicating some transaction was required. An inter-departmental email caught his eye and he quickly opened it.

Your housing loan has been approved and all the details have been forwarded to your accountant for him to take the necessary action. Congratulations on your new apartment. You can move in any time from now. Keys are with Special Agent Steve Goodall.

Reuben typed back, *Thanks*.

Nine o'clock clicked by and Reuben's phone rang. It was

the front desk.

"We have a man here who says he has an appointment to see you. His name is Pasquale Fernandez."

"That is correct. Send him down."

"Will do."

"Pasquale is here and on his way," Reuben quietly said to Raheem. "You ready to begin your new life?"

"Absolutely."

A knock on the door followed.

"Come in Pasquale," said Reuben extending his hand. Pasquale responded almost warmly. "I think you already know Raheem Komani. He will be representing you later in the day as he now works for The Department."

"From the driving school?" Pasquale couldn't hide his surprise.

"That's right," said Raheem. "I've enrolled to complete my law degree at the university while being employed here."

Turning to Reuben, Pasquale asked, "Do you know what happened last night? I turned my phone off and did what you suggested."

"Good. I'd say keep it off for the time being too. I haven't heard anything of the robbery as yet. Maybe they didn't go through with it?"

"No, they were going to do it alright. With or without me."

Raheem interjected. "Where are you up to with filling out the details of your involvement with the gang? I will be saying to the judge that you were informing on them so as not to go further into a life of crime and that you are prepared to do community service on the weekends in lieu of prison time."

"I wrote some things. Here it is," Pasquale said as he handed a scruffy dog-eared piece of paper over to Raheem.

"Thanks, let me study this and work out a strategy."

"Pasquale, stay cool and wait for us in the foyer while we sort through a few things. We won't be long," said Reuben pointing to the corridor.

"Ok," said Pasquale, a slightly apprehensive look crossing his face as he closed the door behind him.

Steve Goodall passed Pasquale on his way to Reuben's office. Goodall knocked on the door and entered.

"Good morning Reuben, was that your robbery informer?"

"Yes it was, his name is Pasquale Fernandez. Boss, let me introduce you to Raheem too."

"I've heard a lot of good things about you, Raheem. Steve Goodall," he said proffering a hand.

"Pleased to meet you sir. It is such an opportunity that I never dreamt would ever come my way and I will do my best to live up to your expectations of me," said Raheem as he shook Steve's hand very firmly.

"I'm sure you will."

"Boss, did anything happen last night?"

"Sure did. The store got messed up a bit but the owner is safe. Two of the assailants were killed and the driver was apprehended. He is due to be before a judge at ten. The same judge has agreed to hear Pasquale's testimony and will be quite sympathetic towards him if he plays it cool."

"Wow! Raheem is going to represent him as I thought it would be a good way to show what he's capable of."

"Fill these forms out first, Raheem, and maybe we can catch up for lunch around one to further chat. Welcome aboard anyway. By the way Reuben, apart from the extra brownie points we are getting from the CPD, here is the key to your new apartment. Move in whenever you like and I would suggest you change the locks and the code for the elevator. I can get one of our junior techs to handle it for you if you like. Just let me know and I'll tee it up. "

"Thanks Boss, I appreciate it."

"Thank you for the forms, one o'clock should be fine, depending on what happens in the courtroom I guess," said Raheem.

"Sounding like a lawyer already," laughed Goodall as he strode out of the office.

Raheem looked over at Reuben with a glint in his eyes as if he still couldn't believe it was really happening for him.

"That was pretty easy."

"Steve is a good guy and loyal to the enth degree when it comes to one of his employees. Let's fill that form out. I reckon you are going to be busy from here on. Did you bring your passport?"

"It's all here," said Raheem opening his briefcase.

Reuben and Raheem studied the security forms first and Raheem knew exactly what to write down. They next filled out the general job application forms for the DA's Department and Raheem whizzed through it without missing a beat.

"You don't need me at all," joked Reuben.

"Oh yes I do."

Reuben's mobile buzzed that a message had come through. It was from Steve Goodall.

Honorable Eugene Williams. George N. Leighton Criminal Court Building, 2600 S. California Avenue, Criminal Division

- Room 101, 9:30. I've booked a cab and just bill it to The Department. Good luck.

"Let's go. There's a cab waiting for us."

Raheem took a moment to calm himself before methodically gathering his papers and following Reuben to the foyer. Pasquale looked up when he saw them; he had a worried look in his eyes. Without a word, Raheem passed his job application papers to the receptionist.

"It's all happening Pasquale, and I think it will be just fine. Stay cool," said Reuben as Raheem nodded in support.

"Did they rob the liquor store?"

"Tried to. No more info at the moment, let's just get this deal sorted out first, ok?"

"I guess so." Pasquale stifled a deep sigh.

As the three men left the building, a taxi pulled up and they all climbed in. The driver had the location details and was soon speeding off down town. Pasquale had his face against the window watching the world flash by and wondering what his life would look like once the judge had made his decision. Raheem rummaged around in his briefcase just making triple sure he had everything while Reuben played around with his new apartment key, putting it on his key ring.

The cab pulled up outside the court building and the driver handed Reuben a chit to sign.

Upon entering the building, and passing the mandatory scanning, they were caught up in a hive of activity. Lawyers and police officers were rushing this way and that, some looking preoccupied, others looking very full of their own importance.

"Room 101?" Reuben asked a security guard.

"Up those stairs. Nothing happening yet though."

"Thanks. I know."

The clock on the wall of the courtroom was just ticking over to nine-thirty as the three men entered and took their seats. Two attendants were busy arranging papers and testing microphones and, even though they were aware that people had come in, continued their pre-court procedures without looking up.

Reuben and Pasquale had never been in a court room before and were quite absorbed in studying different aspects of the scenario. Raheem was taking in some deep breaths trying to compose himself once more. Suddenly, Judge Williams appeared from a back door and installed himself regally on the throne of his office. The court attendants were taken by surprise, having not been informed of the earlier scheduling of the session.

"All rise for the Honorable Judge Williams. Court is now in session," announced an attendant, reciting the words so well known in all courtrooms throughout the country.

The three men rose and faced the judge.

"I'm not sure who these people are, judge," said the attendant.

"That's alright Paul. I'm assuming you are from the DA's Department and I'm to hear a testimony from a Pasquale Fernandez. Who is representing him?" asked the judge looking directly at Reuben.

"I am," said Raheem confidently. "Raheem Komani, your honour."

"Proceed."

"My client has been involved in petty thieving over the

past twelve months and is quite remorseful that his life had drifted down that path. His mother died some two years ago and his brother is serving in the marines. When all this came about, Pasquale was feeling quite abandoned and angry at the world. Even though he was, and still is, employed as an automobile mechanic, three people from a very different set of circumstances, persuaded him to earn some extra money by petty thieving at night. When it was suggested that it was time to up the ante and attempt a hit on a working business using firearms, my client decided that he would not participate in any further acts of crime and made contact with The District Attorney's Office to inform us that an attempt would be made on Greeks Liquor Store."

"I see," said Williams, in an impartial voice.

Raheem pressed on. "We contacted the Police Department immediately and officers staked out the premises and thus averted any harm coming to the owner. Two of the criminals were killed in the incident and one, the driver I believe, was arrested and is due to appear here in this court later in the morning."

Pasquale visibly tensed upon hearing of the death of his former partners-in-crime.

"There is a lot of crime going on in Chicago at the moment and examples must be made, you understand," said the judge looking at the now pale, distressed face of Pasquale.

"Yes, your honour," continued Raheem, "but in this case I would ask for some leniency as my client has actively shown by his forthright actions that he has turned a corner from wrong doings and is prepared to repay society, rather than waste time and money with a prison sentence which I believe would serve no benefit to him or to the public in general.

Allowing him to resume his occupation as a mechanic, as well as weekend duties for the State for as long as you decree reasonable, in lieu of incarceration, I believe would serve the State better and give the right message that it is possible to change for the better."

The judge had a stern look on his face as he pondered the situation. He then indicated to Pasquale to stand up.

"I had been made aware of your circumstances by The District Attorney and, as your council has eloquently stated, there would be no real value to the community by putting a black mark against your name. I will assign my clerk to contact you by mail with the time and place of your community service. I suggest you consider yourself very fortunate at this time. I do not want to see you again in this court for any violation of the trust I have shown in you today. You understand that I will be talking a prison term if you offend again?"

"Yes sir. Thank you."

"Alright, I am satisfied that justice has been served. Case dismissed, " Williams pronounced, gathering up his papers.

"All rise!" shouted the clerk as the judge disappeared swiftly back into his ante-chamber.

Reuben patted Raheem on the shoulder and then gave Pasquale an affirming squeeze on the arm.

"Let's get out of here before he changes his mind," said Reuben, hoping his attempt at a joke would break the tension still apparent on the faces of Raheem and Pasquale.

"Thanks for everything," said Pasquale to Raheem while staring at Reuben, still not quite understanding how it had all come about.

"You are welcome," said Raheem. "My first win too."

Back at the morgue, Pasquale jumped into his car and drove back to his work, feeling the load lifted and knowing he had just ducked a bullet. Raheem and Reuben wandered in the front door, this time, making sure the guards knew who Raheem was before heading to Reuben's office.

"I'll arrange for a laptop so you can write out a full report of the hearing. You were very impressive, I can tell you that," said Reuben, admiration in his voice.

"I actually enjoyed it a lot."

"Reuben Cohn. Could you send a laptop up to my office as soon as possible? Thanks," said Reuben on his phone to the receptionist.

Reuben started to fiddle with his key ring and wondered what his new life would be like in the apartment. His thoughts drifted to Jasmine and how important she had become to him in such a relatively short space of time. Suddenly his phone buzzed and, seeing it was from his mother, he answered it.

"Hi Mum, how are you doing?"

"Not too bad, dear. I was wondering if you would like to have dinner with us again on Friday night."

"Sounds good to me."

"Please bring your girlfriend if you like. She is very welcome, you know."

"Thanks Mum, I will."

"It was Hannah, wasn't it?"

"Not any more, I have a more serious relationship with Jasmine. I'm sure you will approve."

"I'm sure I will. What happened to Hannah, if I may ask?"

"She didn't turn out to be the girl I thought she could have been. Ancient history now, that's for sure. See you Friday."

"Looking forward to it dear, bye."

Raheem picked up on hearing Jasmine's name.

"She is a very special girl. Never understood what she saw in Pasquale, but I'm no expert on women," laughed Raheem, his big teeth enjoying the space outside of his mouth.

"You are right there. Very special."

A brand new laptop suddenly appeared on Reuben's desk. It had been delivered by a junior member of The Department but neither Reuben nor Raheem had noticed him come in with it. Reuben passed the laptop over to Raheem who immediately fired it up and set about personalising the machine, before embarking upon his report.

Reuben had received several online documents relating to his new apartment and the way the finance would be structured. So it was a matter of studying the details, filling out forms and emailing them back. It was quite straightforward but demanded a lot of attention to detail.

Two hours passed in a companionable silence, where the only sounds were the clicking of computer keys.

"You guys ready for a bite?" came from nowhere as Steve Goodall poked his head into the office.

"I reckon I could do with it," said Reuben, looking questioningly over at Raheem.

"There's more to write but it can wait, I guess."

"Good! We'll take my car," suggested Goodall.

Steve Goodall was always happy to share his prized automobile with like-minded souls. He knew Reuben loved it and guessed, correctly, that Raheem would enjoy the power and speed as well. Reuben took the somewhat cramped position in the backseat to let Raheem soak up the pleasure of riding up front.

Goodall revved the engine whenever he could and spun the wheels a couple of times on purpose as the car obeyed every command. It clung to the road through the wet conditions and Steve performed wheelies to thrill the passengers. The normally mild-mannered Steve Goodall was in his element.

As the Porsche zoomed past *Henry's*, Reuben had no idea where they were being taken for lunch so he sat back, as best he could, and enjoyed the ride. Fifteen minutes later, Goodall pulled up outside a group of factories and pointed to one of them.

"Sunshine Oil."

"Oh, and the other one?" asked Reuben, remembering that Domenicci had two distributors for his oil. He peered out the window at the workers coming and going, imagining they were all totally oblivious to the nefarious activities going on under their noses.

"About three minutes away. I'll show you."

Goodall revved the engine once again and zipped through some back streets. He knew where he was going. It looked like he had studied the routes to the factories and Domenicci's home.

They were soon in an easy viewing position of a group of shops that looked quite normal in this part of town. Goodall pointed to one of them.

"Sicilian Oil. Much smaller isn't it?"

"I guess we'll know more after tomorrow. Do you know what time the boat docks?" queried Reuben.

"Five-thirty in the morning. The *Kuta Baru*, last port Catania. Unloading and customs could take a few days but I'm guessing things will move a lot, lot, quicker for Domenicci. The FBI have already staked the place so we will wait until they inform us of the actual pick-up. It's their deal now, pretty much, but they want you and me on hand when they do the raids. Ok?"

"Sure Boss. I mean, Domenicci already knows about us wouldn't you think?"

"I'd say so. He'd be waiting for the shipment too before he goes after us and Hamilton to clean up the loose ends," said Goodall with a wry smile on his face. "And we'll be ready for him, so don't worry too much at the moment."

Reuben didn't respond but kept his eyes on the storefront as Goodall drove past it. Once he had driven a block away, he spun the car around and headed back towards the morgue. Light rain had started to fall but the Porsche disregarded the slippery conditions and gripped the road like a tiger on the prowl.

Familiar suburbs clicked into view and there it was, *Henry's*, Goodall's favourite diner was nearly full up with hungry burger lovers. Reuben was glad to be out of the back seat and stretched his cramped limbs, sucking in the crisp air.

"That feels better."

The three musketeers trooped inside and found places at the bar. Goodall caught Henry's eye and winked at him.

"Three specials Henry!"

"Coming up Steve."

Raheem had been very quiet during the ride and was deep in thought. Reuben picked up on Raheem's mood, and patted him reassuringly on the shoulder.

"I bet you are feeling the sudden change. Am I right?"

"It was not something I had time to properly prepare myself for. I like to think things through and then take some time to act out whatever it is in a measured fashion. This was definitely not on my radar."

"You're not unhappy about it though?"

"Of course not. I love it. It's just sinking in," said Raheem with a smile returning to his face.

"Good," chimed in Goodall. "I've got a good feel about you already. I'm sure you'll fit in with us like a hand in a glove."

"I hope so."

Lunch passed amiably, with the three colleagues chatting easily about the joy of fast cars, Reuben's imminent licence test, and the undisputed supremacy of Henry's burgers.

Goodall zoomed them back to the morgue and then promptly disappeared. Raheem settled in to finishing his report, rewriting it several times before he was happy that it reflected exactly what had transpired. He knew it was only a test case and that no follow-up would be required as far as Pasquale was concerned. Pasquale was now on his own and no doubt even he realized that.

Back in his well-worn, oil-smeared overalls, spanner in hand, Pasquale couldn't stop mulling over the recent events. He thought of Jasmine, and how badly he had treated her. This weird dude Reuben, who had incredibly saved him, now also made it impossible for there ever to be another chance with the wondeful woman he had lost. His mind then turned to .his former "buddies" who were now either dead or incarcerated and how lucky he was to have escaped the situation he had been in only a few days earlier.

Pasquale made a solemn vow to himself that he would keep his head down for the rest of his life and never stray from that path once his community service time had been completed. This had been a life lesson he had taken to heart.

Relishing what he knew to be the last days of his former work life, Reuben went to work on analysing a bone fragment that had been delivered that morning. It was nothing too dramatic, thankfully, just a bone from a stray dog that had been incinerated in a house fire. The circumstances of the fire, however, were suspicious but the dog had nothing to add to the mystery. Reuben's formal report assessed that the dog had died from the obvious cause of being in the wrong place at the wrong time. After placing the fragment back into the cylinder and then the refrigerated cabinet, Reuben emailed the officer responsible for the investigation with his report.

Raheem had finished his courtroom report. He was a little curious as to what Reuben actually did for The Department, but he said nothing.

"I have a favour if you don't mind?" asked Reuben.

"Sure, what is it?"

"Help me move some clothes from my old apartment into the new one."

"No problem. When do you want to do it?"

"Right now if you like. I'm sure you won't be expected to do anything else except get your books and start studying. So you won't be missed around here for the time being."

"I was wondering what I should be doing. Ok let's do it then."

Reuben tidied his desk, locked up his office and the two of them went out the side exit to where Raheem's car was parked. Luckily, thought Reuben, it was a station wagon, a Ford, that had a few scratches on the bodywork. Reuben took a good look at the car, pretty much for the first time, because a few days back he hadn't really observed it. Reuben thought of what car he might eventually end up with, and, though he liked the practicality of the wagon, he discounted the idea straight away. He would prefer to drive Jasmine around in a car that was a bit more flashy than that.

"You lived here?" asked an astounded Raheem as they entered the front door of the old apartment.

"It doesn't look much now," Reuben chuckled and then added, "It never looked any good, really."

A suitcase crammed with clothes and two boxes of canned goods and toiletries were all that were pushed and dragged outside. Reuben did a last check of the apartment and muttered a goodbye under his breath, then locked the door, never to return.

"Is this all?"

"I travel light," Reuben replied. "I've already disposed of the big stuff and the table can stay. I don't really want to be reminded that I lived in such a crappy place. This is the past."

A quarter of an hour later, Reuben was showing Raheem his new apartment.

"Wow!"

"I hope Jasmine likes it."

"Who wouldn't like this?" Raheem said with his mouth still wide open.

After delivering his meagre belongings to his new home,

Reuben had Raheem drop him back at the driving school. He was about to go in when his phone rang. It was Steve Goodall.

"Hey Reuben, the *Kota Baru* is docking at about four in the morning and we have plenty of FBI men sniffing in all directions."

"Do you want me to do anything?"

"Not yet. I think in a couple of days when we move in you might be useful in getting more info from whoever we arrest."

"Sounds good to me."

"Oh yeah, I just heard through the grapevine that Hamilton killed himself. Can't say I'm sorry. I don't actually believe it; old man Domenicci was pretty consistent in tying up loose ends, so I'm guessing this is young Alberto making a statement, if you know what I mean."

"Should I be concerned?" asked Reuben nervously.

"We should have him before he tries anything more with us, but I've had The FBI put a couple of guys watching out for you, and me, for that matter. Strictly precautionary. Better safe than sorry, as my dad used to say."

"Thanks Steve."

"Speak to you later when things happen," he said and the line clicked off.

Reuben was instantly alarmed and some of the colour in his face drained out. He felt a little ill as well but managed to compose himself before he walked inside to meet up with Jasmine.

She was waiting for him, tidying the office area, and had a warm smile on her face when he walked through the door.

They embraced and kissed. She noticed he was a bit tense and he picked up on her reaction.

"A tough day alright, but I feel better now," he said, forcing a smile.

"Did Pasquale turn up?"

"Yes and Raheem spoke to the judge on his behalf."

"Raheem?"

"He was quite amazing. It was like he was made for it. The judge gave Pasquale a two-year good behavior bond – no conviction – but he has to do weekend work when given the order."

"Raheem did all that for him? He never liked Pasquale, you know."

"I know, he told me. Raheem's got a real professional manner. He's gonna make a great lawyer, I know it. This was a bit like a test and he passed with flying colours. You ready to see the new apartment?"

"Sure am."

Jasmine locked up the office and they strolled, arm in arm, down the road. For both of them, it felt like they had known each other for a lot longer than they actually had.

"My mother invited us over to dinner on Friday night if that's ok with you?" Reuben said with a sparkle in his eyes.

"I'd love to meet your parents. I bet they won't like the idea that I'm not Jewish," she said questioningly.

"The only thing that matters to my mum is that you're a good person and that you make me feel happy. I can tell you that those boxes are fully ticked, as far as I'm concerned."

"What about your dad?"

"Even I haven't got a handle on him at the moment. I'm hoping he's got other things to distract him. He's been a bit hard on my mum of late but she's taking it very well. Retirement can do that to lots of people but I'm working on a couple of strategies to ease the tension a bit. Hope so."

Reuben pointed to the apartment block with a grin.

"Hope you will like it."

Jasmine was wide-eyed as they went up in the elevator, and even more so when Reuben opened the double door and ushered her in.

"You have to be kidding with me!" she exclaimed with some glee in her voice.

"Me and the bank now own it. You like?"

"You bet!"

Reuben moved one of his boxes of clothes to one side and took Jasmine by the hand to gaze out onto the street below. There was her driving school office in plain sight and *Henry's* as well. Reuben allowed her to wander through the kitchen and bedrooms, letting her take it all in at her own pace.

"I'd really like this to be our home, if you know what I mean? What do you say?"

"Are you asking me to marry you?" she said half-jokingly.

"If you'll have me."

Jasmine looked at him incredulously. Reuben sensed that, since she left Lebanon, her life had been stuck in a holding pattern and that she felt that true happiness would never come her way because she had deserted the homeland she loved. She felt she didn't deserve to find happiness. Reuben held her tightly and whispered in her ear.

"It's our new beginning. Just you and me. The past is what it is and I don't expect you to forget any part of it, but a person can't live in the past. I'm asking you to share the present with me and maybe have a family of our own sometime down the track."

These were the words that Jasmine had dreamt of hearing and yet it was a little overwhelming and intimidating to her. She pulled out of his clutches and stared blindly out of the window.

"It's so fast," she said softly. "We barely know each other. I'm scared, too, that I won't measure up to who you think I am."

"I know who you are and where you've come from. I know that I love you and I believe you love me as well. You do don't you?"

"I do love you."

"Well, just trust me."

"I do trust you," she said and nestled into his chest, like a cat near a fireplace.

Reuben could feel her heart pounding, as his was, and he held her tightly. The heavens opened up, as if on cue, with a flash of lightning and a couple peals of thunder as they watched the rain wash their past away as it fell on the street below.

As they walked hurriedly back down the wet street, the lure of *Henry's* was irresistible. Reuben had taken his suit coat off and used it as an umbrella to shield Jasmine from the rain. There was no discussion between them as they went in and sat at the bar. Busy as ever, Henry looked up and was genuinely pleased to see them.

"Better in here, I'd say. Your usual?"

"Why not," said Reuben smiling at Jasmine who nodded her approval.

Reuben had the good sense not to pressure Jasmine. They ate their dinner companionably, and chatted about the day's events, with particular emphasis upon Raheem's stellar turn in the courtroom, and Pasquale's relief at the outcome.

After dinner, Reuben and Jasmine walked briskly through a break in the rain back to her place.

Exhausted but exhilarated, Reuben leant over to kiss Jasmine goodnight. He sensed she was not going to sleep any time soon; her busy brain was mulling over her apartment, and making not-so-subtle comparisons to Reuben's new luxurious abode. He took the opportunity to re-open the topic without being too pushy.

"What do you say about giving up the lease on this place and moving in with me? You could put your own feel to whatever you think needs changing. I mean, why waste money on rent?"

"I know it all sounds logical. Can I sleep on it for a bit?"

"Of course."

Reuben let her nestle into his chest and he spent the next hour listening to her breathing. Even though it was quite early in the evening, Jasmine slept soundly, perhaps for the first time since she left Lebanon. She moved position a few times through the night, but tended to drift back into Reuben's chest. a position they now both felt totally comfortable with.

Jasmine was up at the crack of dawn. Small shafts of sunlight snuck through the joins of the curtains and shone directly on her face. She freed herself and gazed at Reuben, still sleeping soundly. Her mind immediately snapped back to his suggestion of the night before, wondering if sharing an apartment was the right thing to do.

Tossing the question over and over in her mind, she couldn't see what the big deal would be if they found out later that they were incompatible. But she knew in her heart that she would do anything and everything to make it work and that Reuben was a good man who she believed would not intentionally harm her. By the time Reuben opened his eyes he knew she had made her decision and was delighted beyond belief.

"This is going to be so special," he said kissing her on the neck, still mindful of the need to give her space, and not force her into pinning down the details of where, how and when.

The *Kota Baru* eased gently into the Calumet Harbour and docked. Everything went according to routine. The dock regulators knew the vessel pretty well as it visited Chicago twice a year and had been doing so since it was built twelve years earlier. The ten-man crew was mainly from South Korea. The captain was a Swedish national, Mika Hendricksen, tall and brawny, well over six feet tall and with scars on his face that indicated he was not a man to be messed with. Hendricksen understood English very well and was quite adept at getting his papers verified by the coast guards, unloading his cargo and replacing it very swiftly. Time was money in his books as he received extra bucks for delivering on time.

These docks were part of the Foreign Trade Zone where a peculiar loophole in the import regulations existed. Due to the fact that certain components from overseas were required by local importers to complete their own products, tariffs were lower, or non-existent. This olive oil had somehow been designated within that category, as it was being rebottled and rebranded in Chicago. The paperwork was genuine and the transaction was legal.

The FBI kept their distance as the container load of crates of bottled oil got hoisted from the ship and deposited onto the empty dock. Almost immediately a forklift appeared and the cargo was soon safely stored in one of the large warehouses. A smartly-dressed man from Sunshine Oil signed the necessary papers and then phoned through to say that the trucks could pick it up.

Tuning in to the signal and locking in to the phone of the Sunshine Oil executive was quite an easy procedure for the FBI. They immediately started to monitor all conversations, not that there was anything incriminating coming from them. The members of Domenicci's crew were far too professional for anything like that. They were always on their guard for the possibility of being bugged by the authorities.

Two trucks rumbled in. On their side panels, they boldly bore the name of Sunshine Oil, along with a risng sun logo. The trucks were soon loaded up and back on their way to the factory, followed at a safe distance by three FBI cars.

The factory was a good hour's journey from the docks. When they finally arrived at the Sunshine Oil factory, it was just after seven in the morning. The trucks made their way through the big gates and six men came out of the office and started unloading.

The three FBI cars suddenly slipped in next to the trucks and ten officers got out. The slick-looking man from the docks saw them. He didn't look pleased to have his supervision of the unloading interrupted.

"What's going on?" he asked quite abruptly.

"Cameron Johnson's my name. FBI," said Cameron showing his badge to the man.

"So? What are you doing here?"

"We have a warrant to search your premises for contraband items," said Cameron, displaying the papers. "What is your name and your position here?"

"Carlo Franetti. I run the workers here. Look around, you won't find anything," he said. Pulling out his mobile phone he immediately called Albert Domenicci. "Alberto, the FBI are here."

"Sit tight and cooperate. I'll handle it."

"Ok Boss."

Over the years, Albert Domenicci had paid a lot of his ill-gotten gains to a select group of officers of the The Chicago Police Department. Now was the time to get a result. Albert calmly phoned his main contact at the CPD, Captain Robert Wilson.

"Robert, Alberto. FBI all over Sunshine Oil. What do you know about it?"

"Nothing. I'll get some boys to go there and check it out."

"You go yourself too, ok?"

"Sure, Alberto. I'll let you know."

Domenicci had known nothing but crime since the day he was born. He had a good criminal pedigree, his father having been one of Chicago's foremost drug-runners in the seventies. Not much fazed Albert. He'd seen it all, and was always on the alert for trouble. He was a man who kept his cool, under any circumstances.

Still in his dressing-gown, Albert phoned his pilot at the

nearby airport to ready his private plane for an immediate takeoff. He then phoned his lawyer, Travis Coffee, who was holidaying with his wife in The Bahamas.

Travis Coffee had always wanted to be a lawyer. The income from his early years had certainly not been a disappointment, but now that such a notable figure as Domenicci was his major client, the sky was the limit. Every year Travis took at least two overseas holidays, always accompanied by his wife. Usually his elderly mother was taken along for the ride.

The Bahamas had always been his favorite destination – an opportunity to just unwind and switch off. His latest trip was barely two days in. Sleeping peacefully, Travis was rudely awakened by the buzz of his mobile phone. The cold voice was unmistakeable.

"Travis, get on a plane now and fly back to Chicago. I'll let you know more details when you land."

"Yes Alberto," said Travis sensing the urgency in Albert's voice.

Albert was not a man to say no to. Travis rang for a taxi, kissed his sleeping wife and raced to the airport. While in the taxi he phoned to find the next plane back home. There was one that left in an hour. He booked it.

The first box of oil had not even made it from the truck through the factory door, when one of the FBI officers called a halt to any further unloading.

Carlo looked on impassively as another of the FBI men took a grip on the box.

"What's in here?"

"Olive oil. See for yourself."

"We will," said the officer.

Pulling out a heavy knife, he yanked the steel staples from the box and sliced through the masking tape.

The bottles were stacked neatly and tightly with six to a carton. Cameron knew what he was looking for.

"I'm going to empty the oil from here. Is there some place I can do that so you can still have the product to reuse?"

"Pour it in here. That will be fine," said Carlos, handing him a bucket. "It's just oil."

"Thanks."

Cameron carefully opened the bottle and poured the contents into the bucket, making sure not to spill any. The oil looked rich and golden as it sat there glinting in the sunlight.

Captain Robert Wilson in a CPD squad car pulled in and made his way aggressively to Johnson.

"Who are you? What's going on?" Wilson demanded.

"Cameron Johnson, FBI, and I'm sure you know what this is," he said showing the search warrant.

"Yeah, well?"

"Routine check, following a tipoff. Domenicci call you?"

"Don't get smart with me buster. This is my town."

"Let's see what we find then, together if you like."

Johnson extracted an odd-looking device from his jacket pocket. Exerting pressure on the handle of the glass-cutter, he started to cut away at the thickest part of the oil bottle.

"What do you expect to find in there?" asked a now nervous Wilson.

The bottom part of the bottle fell away as neatly as if a

surgeon had done it in an operation. Two plastic bags fell out. Johnson looked at Wilson with a grin.

"Why don't you take a look? It sure doesn't look like any oil that I've seen before."

Wilson tentatively picked up one of the bags and broke its seal. Out came a white powder. Everyone who'd ever worked in drug enforcement recognised it as pure heroin. Johnson touched some of the powder and then licked it.

"What do you think Captain?" asked Cameron sarcastically.

"What do you think?"

"I think Alberto has a few problems that even you won't be able to cover for, don't you? You better phone it in to the station and to Domenicci. I'm going to need to have a chat with him. See if you can arrange it, will you?"

"What makes you think I've got an in with him!" Wilson exclaimed defensively. "I don't know what he's up to."

"Of course you don't! Well, he's going to suspect somebody I reckon," laughed Johnson. "I wouldn't be you for quids, if you get my drift."

Wilson threw a black look at Johnson, and, taking out his cellphone to report in to Domenicci and his CPD superiors, muttered under his breath, "Fuck you too!"

Johnson phoned Steve Goodall with the news.

"Steve, your man was right on the money."

"Drugs?"

"In the first bottle of oil anyway. We'll take the whole shipment to our factory and go through it with a fine tooth comb. Tell that guy of yours, if he ever needs a job, I'll give him one. He's the real deal alright."

"I'll tell Reuben you said hi," laughed Goodall. "He's going back to school, would you believe, to become a doctor."

"You don't say!"

"Yep. Top guy alright."

"Got plenty to do here. Catch you later Steve."

"Thanks Cameron. I'd say we're sort of even now."

Cameron Johnson was an experienced operator in the field of drug busts. Even though no-one had made any threatening moves as yet, Cameron knew something could happen at any moment. His men had already been prepared for a potential fight, at the ready with their shotguns out and loaded. Cameron urged them to stay on the alert, while he phoned the headquarters of the FBI and asked for more backup. He then addressed Carlos.

"This place is in lockdown and you will need to make a statement as to your involvement in all of this. Anything you say now will be taken and used against you in a court of law. You are allowed to speak to a lawyer. Do you understand your rights?"

"I'm not saying nothing." Carlos looked stubbornly defiant.

"Ok. Carlos Franetti, I'm arresting you on suspicion of importing or assisting in importing drugs. Show me your hands."

Carlos offered his hands as casually as if he'd done it many times before. Johnson cuffed him and led him to one of the FBI cars. Another police car pulled up as well as a van with National Guardsmen in it. Both police cars watched on in silence as the FBI men reloaded the trucks with the boxes of oil and eventually drove them out of the premises.

It seemed like it was over for the moment. The National Guardsmen climbed back into their vans and drove off.

Albert Domenicci dressed more hurriedly than usual. He threw a few essentials into his overnight holdall, and withdrew a stack of one-hundred dollar bills from the safe hidden in his closet. Firing up the silver Mercedes, he sped across town to a private airstrip.

As he screeched to a halt, he could see the four-seater Cessna 172 sitting on the tarmac. His faithful pilot had the plane idling, ready for a hasty take-off.

As Domenicci scrambled up the steps and threw himself into a seat, the pilot casually asked, "Where to Alberto?"

"Mexico City," commanded Albert, internally breathing a sigh of relief.

"Sorry boss, not enough gas. We'll need to refuel in Houston."

Domenicci hid his annoyance, but there was nothing that could be done about it. The little plane took to the skies and headed south. Three hours later they touched down at a Houston cargo air strip to refuel.

Looking out the window, Domenicci felt his blood run cold. The car on the tarmac bore ominously government-style plates. Barely a few moments passed before two heavily armed FBI agents boarded the plane.

"What the fuck . . ." Domenicci muttered angrily under his breath; even he had been caught by surprise.

In what seemed like a mirror rerun of Cameron Johnson arresting Carlos back at Sunshine Oil, the ever-efficient FBI officers read Domenicci his rights, slapped him in handcuffs, and flew him back to Chicago in one of their own planes. Not a shot had been fired.

Jasmine had made sunny-side-up eggs on toast with steaming coffee. The whole domestic situation was still so surreal for Reuben – something he had often dreamt about but never thought would actually happen for him.

He had switched his mobile phone to silent during the night, and even though he heard a buzz every so often, he was determined not to shift his focus from Jasmine. Everything else could wait. The clock on the wall chimed away to indicate nine o'clock. Jasmine and Reuben looked at each other in some alarm.

"We're late!" Jasmine gently exclaimed, not really wanting to stir from the romance of the moment.

"I know. Let's get going. Tomorrow night at my place, ok?"

"Ok."

They both scrambled to get their shoes and coats on and literally raced out the door. Luckily the rain had passed as they ran to where Jasmine worked.

A hurried peck on the lips and Reuben's long strides soon had him in the front entrance of the morgue. Racing past the new guards and into his office, he plonked himself down, quite out of breath. Raheem was already there, and gave him a knowing look. Reuben finally checked his mobile phone to find a message from Steve.

The operation went well. You were right about the bottles. Cameron has impounded the whole container load; it could be quite a haul. Domenicci tried to leave the country but we nabbed him in Houston. Give me a call when you can. Steve.

"Hi Raheem, how are you doing?"

"Not as good as you, it appears. What do you think I will be expected to do today? Do you know?"

"Good question. I'll ask Steve," said Reuben as he clicked onto Steve's number.

"Hi Reuben, another good job I'd say," said Steve.

"Thanks Boss. I was wondering if you needed either Raheem or me for anything in particular or would it be alright if we started on our prep work for the university?"

"No, I think that would be in order. I could always call you in if an occasion arises, couldn't I?"

"Of course. By the way, is it possible for you to arrange that locksmith you mentioned the other day to come over to my new place and change the locks and make up two sets of keys?"

"I'll get onto it right away. He'll text you when he's about to head down to the apartment."

"Thanks Boss, we will talk later, no doubt."

"Study hard," said Goodall as the phone went dead.

"It's all good. We can do our own thing until called for action," said Reuben to Raheem.

"That's so good. I'll pick you up on Friday morning, if you like, and we can get our books."

"Nine-thirty would be perfect, after I walk Jasmine to work."

"I'll see you then," said Raheem as he took his briefcase and left the office.

Reuben felt a slight pang of abandonment as he had become used to Raheem and his quirky remarks over the past two days. Reuben, who had always worked alone, actually enjoyed having him there smiling with his big teeth.

He knew that Raheem had his own things to organize and that he was keen to reacquaint himself with some other Syrian refugees. Not only would Raheem share his good news with them, but he would let them know that he was available should they need any legal advice. Raheem was very fastidious about doing what he believed was the right thing. It's what got him into trouble with the Syrian authorities in the first place. That part of him was never going to change.

Reuben locked up his office and wandered down to the street. He strolled past *Henry's* and Jasmine's office as well as his new apartment. A block further along was a large supermarket and it had occurred to Reuben that he should stock up on a few basic things, like milk and cheese, so that Jasmine felt at home. She had cooked for him and he really wanted to try something in that arena, no matter how terribly it might turn out. There was always *Henry's* if the worst came to the worst.

A few mothers pushing trolleys, some with babies in them, some with food items, were the only customers at that time. Reuben pushed his trolley and soon had it half-filled with all sorts of interesting things. Soft toilet paper was one thing he had noticed at Jasmine's and he much preferred it to the hard, single ply, cheaper brand that he usually bought. Brightly-coloured tissues and disposable napkins, something he never bought, adorned his trolley too. He consciously observed other people's purchases, some of which gave him good ideas. *Jasmine will be impressed*, he thought as he went from aisle to aisle.

Soon his trolley was full. He'd even added a slow-cooker which had caught his eye.

Heading to the checkout, he asked the friendly assistant

if she would keep an eye on his purchases, while he made another circuit of the store.

"No problem at all. We are here to serve you."

Reuben smiled as he pondered what he would attempt to cook that night for Jasmine. There were helpful cards on that subject, strategically placed around the store, and he soon had a tidy collection of them. Spaghetti Bolognaise looked the simplest and most likely to succeed, so he bought some multi-coloured pasta, minced beef, cooking oil, a jar of the Paul Newman sauce that just required a bit of heating, two onions and a clove of garlic. The instructions were very clear on how many minutes the pasta should be cooked for and that it was very important to drain the hot water once taken from the stove and rinse thoroughly with cold water to avoid the pasta sticking together and over cooking.

A fresh and crispy French stick seemed like a good idea and pretty soon he was at the checkout paying two hundred and thirty-three dollars and sixty-five cents from his credit card.

"I've never spent this much on food, ever," he explained to the girl.

"It's quite normal if you're just newly setting up your house, as you appear to be doing."

"That's exactly what I'm doing," he replied, thinking how smart and observant she was.

Realizing he could never grapple this collection home without a car, he enquired if all his goods could be delivered and at what time he would get them.

After ascertaining his address, the checkout girl replied, "Eleven-thirty, because you are only a block away. Is that alright sir?"

"Perfect. Thank you."

As Reuben left the store, his mobile phone buzzed with a text message.

Hi Reuben, is it ok to swing by your place in half an hour to do the new locks? Bob Henderson.

Great. Thanks Bob, Reuben texted back.

He knew that it wouldn't take him too long to get back to the apartment but he picked up his step and made it in good time. There was a man about to go into the elevator and Reuben called to him.

"Bob!"

"No, who are you?" replied the man.

"I live here," said Reuben.

"So do I. haven't seen you before though. Travis Coffee. Did you take the old lady's unit?" he said extending a hand.

"That's right. Reuben." The two men shook hands.

Travis was about five foot ten and of very solid build. Dark hair and tanned complexion. From the handshake, Reuben learnt that Travis had been on holiday with his wife and mother in The Bahamas and had been called back suddenly early this morning at the request of a client. Reuben couldn't quite get a handle on the nature of the client.

"I'm getting the locks changed. You can't be too careful, can you?"

"Pretty quiet around here though."

"Maybe a drink later in the week?" suggested Reuben, who was now curious to know more about this man.

"See how I go. I'll knock on your door when I get a window."

"Sounds good," said Reuben and patted him on the shoulder.

With that touch, the nature of Travis Coffee's work, and his client, was instantly revealed. *What a small world*, thought Reuben. Travis was a lawyer, and obviously doing well for himself, judging by the images Reuben was gleaning of a smart modern office uptown. There was a lot going on in Travis's mind. Foremost amongst it was Alberto Domenicci.

A tradesman's van pulled up and a lean, scruffy, guy in overalls got out and made his way to the two men. He looked about the same height as Reuben and had a baseball cap firmly planted on his head. Wisps of blond hair could be seen trying to break free.

"Must be your locksmith. See you around," said Coffee, heading into the elevator. Reuben watched as the illuminated numbers indicated that Travis lived on the top floor.

"Hi Bob," said Reuben. "I love punctuality."

"Steve Goodall told me to do an extra special job for you and send him the bill. Let's get to it then."

It was obvious that Bob was an expert in his field. After inspecting the elevator security system, and Reuben's unusual double front door arrangement, Bob turned to Reuben with casual confidence.

"Too easy. How many copies of the keys do you want?"

"Two sets would be fine. Will it take long?"

"Twenty minutes, give or take. I'll get my gear."

They both took the elevator back to the ground floor and Reuben handed Bob his door key.

"You take this and dispose of it. I need to wait for a delivery."

"Ok."

Right on eleven-thirty a young guy from the supermarket

turned up in a van with numerous bags and boxes. Reuben was surprised afresh at the quantity of groceries and other homewares he'd bought. Leaving them outside the elevator he headed up the stairs to find Bob doing the finishing touches to the locks.

"Just about done. I've programmed the lift to have a new password. Nice and simple, 6789, you can change it anytime you like, just call me if you can't work it out yourself."

"Thanks Bob, I'll be fine. Two sets of keys?"

"Yep, on your kitchen table. All finished now, see you."

"Thanks Bob."

Reuben immediately put one set of keys onto his key ring and went back for the shopping. He then stacked all the cool goods into the large refrigerator, but it still looked very empty. He wrote a little list onto his phone to remind himself of further possible purchases. Reuben suddenly decided it was easier to lunch at *Henry's* and do the rest of the unpacking later in the afternoon.

A short walk and he was in familiar surroundings eating his free burger. As he ate, still aware of the constant need to refine his slow-eating technique, one thought preoccupied his mind: Travis Coffee. Reuben knew that the only person he could talk to about his new neighbor was Steve.

Back in the apartment, Reuben made a thorough inspection of every nook and cranny to see what the old lady had left behind that might be useful. There was another slow cooker that looked a bit more upmarket than the one he had just purchased. *Maybe he could give the one he had just bought to Raheem.* There were plenty of jars of all sorts of spices, along with dishes and utensils of all description: skillets, plates and silverware that appeared brand new. There was even a wok.

Reuben installed his new purchases alongside the things he had inherited from Mrs. Willis. There was plenty of storage space to accommodate all of Jasmine's kitchen wares if she chose to bring them, as he hoped she would. Unpacking his meagre possessions did not take much time at all and he pondered the fact that he'd had so little need of things up to this point in his life. Now it was all different. The tectonic plates had definitely shifted.

Tears streamed from his eyes as he cut and finely diced the onions. Despite the unfamiliar stinging, Reuben persevered through the pain. Putting some cling-wrap over the results of his toil, he stowed the onion in the fridge. Having Jasmine around during the final cooking assault was a planned tactic. She could direct him if he was steering into dangerous territory. He did not want to ruin any of the implements if he could help it.

Five o'clock came and Reuben chose a large saucepan to boil the water. Always eager to be a good student, he followed the recipe to the letter of the law, adding salt and oil. Soon the pot was bubbling excitedly, and he added the spaghetti. The water had receded due to evaporation so Reuben intuitively boiled a kettle and filled the pot back up to the original level. Preventing the strands from sticking together was a bit of a challenge but he achieved it by occasionally grabbing six strands and separating them by hand. Hot work. He was glad Jasmine didn't see him do this as he was quite sure there was a better technique. Confidence was high that at least this part of the operation was doable without destroying too much of the product. It was all so new and exciting.

He let twelve minutes elapse then drained the spaghetti into the colander, scraping off the strands that had stuck ferociously to the bottom of the pan. He ran cold water through the colander, as the recipe had instructed. Time to collect Jasmine.

Reuben had purposely not contacted her during the day and she also hadn't made any attempt to communicate. They both understood that business hours should not be mixed with personal space and time. She was good like that. Even though he secretly wished to chat with her, he realized that absence makes the heart grow fonder and that he had plenty of time when they were alone to make up for it.

As Reuben arrived at the front door of her office, Jasmine was emerging onto the street. She looked a little surprised to see him but smiled warmly.

"I was planning to go to your place and surprise you."

"Our place, I hope," said Reuben giving her a hug.

"We'll see."

Arm in arm they walked back to the apartment. It only took seven minutes. The weather was in a strange holding pattern where the air was very still and dry. Most unusual. Jasmine's flat was about the same distance further away so in her mind it was on her way. Reuben picked up on it and whispered in her ear.

"You know I know what you're thinking. Trust me. It is the right thing to be doing at this wonderful time. We both love each other."

"It's sometimes a little concerning to me that you know me so well. I can't keep any secrets from you, but you can from me."

"I know. I have sort of a secret."

"Yes?"

"I'm cooking dinner for you," he giggled. "I really hope it works out too."

"There's always *Henry's*," she laughed playfully.

"Exactly what I thought too."

Once in the apartment, Jasmine raced over to the window and looked down at the street.

"I simply love this view. I don't think I'll ever tire of it."

"I hope not," whispered Reuben snuggling up behind her and pressing into her body.

Jasmine turned and kissed him on the lips.

"How was your day?"

"Well, the boss gave Raheem and me time to organize ourselves so he did what he did and I explored the cupboards here, packed my stuff away and went shopping for all sorts of things, and then started preparing dinner for us. Met one of our neighbours, Travis Coffee, a lawyer on the top floor. Do you want to come and help me finish the dinner?"

"Sure. What is it?"

"Spaghetti Bolognaise. I hope you'll like it."

"We'll see," she said trying not to hurt his feelings.

Reuben got the onions from the fridge and selected a pan he thought would do the job. Jasmine thought otherwise.

"Let me see," she said as she rummaged through the drawer where all the skillets were sitting.

"My, you got a lot of them."

"Mostly the old lady's."

"This one will be better," she said handing him a larger pan that had a non-stick coating on it.

Jasmine obviously won the kitchen contest hands down;

many more years of experience, but she appreciated Reuben's efforts and was confident he would be a good student. After an hour of frying, sizzling, letting the meat cook in the sauce, and general chit-chat, she announced it was time for the finishing touches.

"We can put the pasta in now if you like."

"Sounds good to me," responded Reuben as he untangled the spaghetti, as best he could, into the pan and mixed it in.

Jasmine selected some large white bowls from the cupboard and placed a fork and spoon on each of two coloured placemats. Reuben brought the pan to the table and sat it on some heat mats. He then got two fancy wine glasses out of a cabinet and proceeded to open a bottle of red wine, pouring some in each.

"Our first meal here," he said proudly as they clinked glasses.

"Tastes good, well done," said Jasmine smiling broadly. "No *Henry's* tonight, I guess?"

"I couldn't have done it without you. Wouldn't have wanted to do it without you. Here's to you, Jasmine."

Reuben's mobile phone buzzed but he ignored it. Nothing was more important than this time with Jasmine.

The old lady had a fancy coffee machine and some unopened coffee beans as well so Reuben brought the instruction manual to the table and they both worked out how to get it happening. It was so much fun doing things together.

After coffee, Reuben enticed Jasmine to the bedroom where they made love and slept soundly in a loving embrace until six in the morning when the work routine, for Jasmine anyway, kicked in. She hurriedly departed, heading home for a fresh set of clothes.

Reuben checked his phone to see that Steve had tried on several occasions to contact him. There was an SMS message. *Call me when you can, nothing urgent. Steve.*

"Hi Boss, just got your message. How are you?"

"Just letting you know that Domenicci had a short hearing yesterday afternoon and bail has been posted so he can defend the accusations."

"Should I be concerned?"

"No, I think he's more worried about the police officers at the CPD who are spilling their guts on him. It's quite amazing. The FBI got all the glory but we all know it was you who cracked the case and nailed him. The trial is in two months but all his oil businesses have been shut down. I'd say he's finished."

"Wow! His lawyer is a neighbour of mine now. Flew back from The Bahamas early yesterday."

"You don't say!"

"By the way, thanks for the locksmith."

"No problem, you deserved it. Speak later, bye."

Reuben had a lot to think about. Foremost was Jasmine. He didn't want Domenicci doing anything crazy and getting Jasmine caught up in it. He decided to tell her everything and let her make her own decision.

Reuben had a good idea that she was already planning to move in over the coming weekend so tonight had to be the time to discuss it.

The day flashed past with trivial achievements. Reuben had pulled out all his first year medical notes and read every word of them. Five years of life experience since then meant that there were many turns of phrase which he now would write differently. The main thing that intrigued him was his almost total recall of the actual time and place that he had written the notes. Some were done in lecture theatres and others at his parents' home.

Thinking back on those university days, he remembered how incredibly focused he had been on the job in hand - there was no idle interest in the opposite sex, even though just under half his class was women. *How things have changed in that area over the past month,* he thought. *Hannah has come and gone and how great it is that I've saved himself for Jasmine. She is simply perfection in a partner and friend.*

Snapping himself out of thoughts of Jasmine, he returned to the lecture notes which had started to take on a new relevance. As a result of his five years of work at the morgue, he had a deeper understanding of anatomical functions and how the body reacted to certain thoughts, releasing chemicals into the bloodstream.

Around five o'clock it felt like he had just completed half a year's refresher course. The alarm on his phone went off to remind him to go down to collect Jasmine. He was not disappointed by the interruption; but rather surprised at the level of his immersion, and thrilled that he would soon be with her again.

Jasmine wanted to get a change of clothes from her place as well as some toiletries so Reuben walked with her and carried two full bags back to his apartment. As they walked, the spitting rain felt quite refreshing to Reuben, but he made sure his umbrella shielded her completely.

He knew that Jasmine disliked the rain. Coming from such a climate as Lebanon, she loved to feel warmth on her body whenever she could. It reminded her of home. The rain had the opposite effect.

Reuben took the opportunity to discuss what had been happening with Domenicci.

"This Domenicci guy worries you a lot, doesn't he?" she asked gently, after he'd explained his concerns in a way he hoped would not excessively alarm her.

"He does. Not for me, though he has a right to be angry at me, but I couldn't bear the thought that you might get caught up in the crossfire."

"I've been in wars before, you know. No-one will ever scare me away from what I want to do and where I want to be again," she said defiantly.

Jasmine made sure that her body touched his as they walked back to the apartment. Reuben knew she felt safe and strong too. He secretly wished that he had never become involved in the world that Domenicci lived in. This was not how he wanted to live.

"What's for dinner?" joked Jasmine. "I'm starving. Missed lunch today because there were too many clients."

"I missed lunch too. How about *Henry's*?"

"Always good to me," she laughed.

On Thursday morning, after dropping Jasmine at work, Reuben took a phone call from Steve.

"Hi Reuben, we have a body part that I'd like you to take a look at if you have the time?"

"Of course, Boss. I'll walk over right now."

It felt familiar and strange, at the same time, as Reuben entered the side entrance of the morgue. He didn't encounter anyone at all as he slipped into his old office and fired up his computer. This was almost like foreign territory now and Reuben knew how far and how fast he had moved on from it. Still, this was his paid job and there was no way he wanted to disappoint Steve. After gloving up, he retrieved the cylinder from the storage fridge and opened it. Inside was part of a severed hand, obviously from an Afro-American person. Before getting the KL33 out, Reuben decided to try touching it to see if he could get anything that way. Taking off the right-handed glove he cautiously placed his hand on the specimen. A wave of fear and sadness swept over him.

"Oh my God!" exclaimed Reuben. "It's one of the black kids."

Reuben dashed outside and hurried to where he had last seen the boys shooting hoops. He sank down with his back to the pole and pondered. *It was only a few days ago that I saw them both here. I wonder what happened to them?* His immediate thought was to text Steve.

Playing a hunch, Boss. Let you know how I go. Reuben.
OK.

Reuben remembered the severed hand was still lying on his desk and so hurried back to his office, hastily placing it back inside the cylinder, inside the fridge. Locking his office, he raced back to the basketball court, where he sat for several hours, waiting and hoping that one of the black kids would turn up.

The odd raindrop fell but no-one came near him, and before he knew it, it was time to collect Jasmine. She immediately noticed the concerned look on his face and asked what was wrong. He explained in detail what he had been doing that day and asked her to come with him to resume the vigil. She agreed, as she could see how important it was for him.

As they neared the area, Reuben noticed someone was now

on the basketball court. It was the black kid to whom he had given the television set a few days earlier. He was alone, shooting hoops and having to fetch each ball when he threw it. Street canny, he spotted Reuben straight away and a smile appeared on his sad face.

"Hey my man, how you doing?"

"I'm ok. This is Jasmine, my fiancé, my name is Reuben, what's yours?" said Reuben extending a hand.

"What you telling this to me for?" asked the young man, a little alarmed.

"Aren't you going to shake my hand? How's the television set going? Still working?"

"Yeah, it's still going good. Jamal," he offered, extending his fist.

Reuben grabbed Jamal's fist and held it tight.

"Where's your friend?"

"I don't know man, why you asking me these things?"

"I know where he is," Reuben said and let the words sink in. "I know that you didn't do it too."

At these words, the lanky teen lost his facade of superiority and bravado. He abruptly sank to his knees sobbing.

"I couldn't help him!"

"I know, you are just a kid and your uncle is a psychopathic killer. I could have had a police van pick you up with all the sirens but I wanted to save you from going to prison, you hear me?"

"How do you know all this? We were alone on his boat."

"Most criminals think that what they are doing is hidden from the authorities. The prisons are full of them. I want you to come with me and make a statement explaining what happened."

"He'll kill me."

"He killed your friend because he was paranoid that he might steal his stash of drugs from the river, didn't he?"

"He came with his fancy car and promised us five hundred bucks each for a couple of hours work. I drove Micah down to the docks where Uncle's boat was and he took us to the other side of the river. Then he asked us to get into these wetsuits and go fetch a box from the bottom. We did it and once we got it on board my uncle pulled out a gun and shot Micah in the head. I didn't know what to do, man. Uncle ordered me to do nothing. He just steered the boat back to where my car was and pushed me out into the water. He threw some money at me but I couldn't touch it. He motored off and I went home. That's it."

"I'm sorry Jamal, it is terrible. There were other boxes down there?"

"About three or four that I saw."

"You must make a statement. Do it for Micah."

Reuben released his hold on Jamal and went back to Jasmine who was shaking with fear.

"Please Jamal," she pleaded. "Reuben is a good man and wants to help you."

"What do you say, Jamal?" said Reuben softly putting his arm around the sobbing young man.

"I'm only eighteen. What could I do?"

"Nothing then. You can do something now before you are in trouble over your head facing long-term prison. Come," said Reuben extending his hand again.

Jamal took Reuben's hand and the three of them walked slowly across the road to the front entrance of the morgue. The guards acknowledged Reuben.

"Is Steve Goodall still in?"

"Yes he is."

"Good, ask him to come down to my office please."

"Sure thing."

Jasmine and Jamal had never been inside a morgue before and it fascinated them both as it distracted their attention from why they were here. Once in Reuben's office, Jamal sat in a chair while Jasmine stood uneasily beside Reuben near his desk.

"What happened to Micah after I left?" asked Jamal.

"Your uncle cut him up and fed him to the fish."

"Oh my God!" shrieked Jasmine, while Jamal stared blankly into space.

"I thought something like that."

Steve Goodall appeared in the doorway.

"What's this all about Reuben?"

"Steve, it's about my hunch on the hand. This is Jamal by the way, he was an eye witness to the murder of his friend, Micah. He wants to make a statement."

"Good work, Reuben. Jamal I must inform you of your rights and that anything you say here could be used against you in a trial. You can have a lawyer present if you want. Do you want one?"

"I want this nightmare over. He was my best friend. I never thought anyone would care if a black kid went missing."

"We care about every citizen here, Jamal," said Goodall

reassuringly. "Give him a pad and pen."

Jamal started writing his statement while Steve, Reuben and Jasmine watched.

"You will be missed around here when you go back to school," whispered Steve to Reuben. "You are a natural field agent if ever I saw one."

"Thanks Boss. I'm going to take Jasmine home now. Big day tomorrow. Is that alright?"

"Sure. I've got it from here."

Jamal noticed that Reuben was about to leave. He stopped his writing and turned around to face him.

"Thank you Reuben. You have saved my life, man. I owe you one."

"You're welcome Jamal. I'm sorry about Micah but that's a done thing. You can have a better life if you can put it behind you, you know?"

"I'll try," said Jamal and turned back to his statement as Reuben and Jasmine left the building.

"That was amazing!" said Jasmine once they were outside. "You are such a good man, Reuben."

They walked arm in arm back down the street that Reuben knew so well. Past *Henry's*, past the driving school, past Good Value Rentals and into the street of their apartment. There were a lot of memories floating in Reuben's head. As they headed to the elevator, a taxi cab pulled up and two women got out. Reuben and Jasmine watched them as the driver put some suitcases on the ground. As one of the women was considerably older than the other, Reuben assessed that they were the wife and mother of Travis Coffee, just back from The Bahamas. So he introduced himself.

"You must be the two Mrs Coffees? We are your new neighbours, Reuben and Jasmine."

"That's correct," said the younger woman. "You must have already met my husband Travis. My name is Rose and my mother-in-law is Shirley. Nice to meet you both."

"Let's do some coffee, excuse the pun, next week if you like?" suggested Reuben.

"Sounds like a good idea, until then," Rose responded.

Jasmine smiled in their direction as they struggled into the elevator with the suitcases.

"Let's walk this time," Jasmine said pointing to the stairs. "A bit crowded in there and I don't like the idea of overloading these things."

"Sounds like a plan," said Reuben as he waved to the women in the elevator and strolled with Jasmine to the stairwell.

"Do you think it's a good idea having a social thing with them?" asked a concerned Jasmine.

"It would look a bit odd if we didn't."

Friday morning, at precisely ten-thirty, a grinning Raheem greeted Reuben at the bottom of the elevator. His smart suit seemed a little out of place as they were only going to the university to collect books and other supplies. Raheem was already playing the lawyer and determined to dress the part at all times. It was something that he had decided was a good habit to get into. Always looking his very best could only get positive professional vibes back from everyone who saw him. Reuben was impressed as well, but had chosen jeans, a heavy woolen shirt, jacket and runners as his attire for the day.

"How have you been going in your new apartment?"

"So far so good. I'm hoping that Jasmine will fully move in with me so that in time we can marry."

"My word, you have moved quickly. She is a lovely woman, there is no doubting that. Have you asked her yet?"

"Actually, I have. I believe she is for it and tonight we are having dinner at my parents' house. Maybe she wants to see what they think about it, her being Muslim and all."

"Yes indeed, I thought along those lines myself. Good luck."

"Thanks, I'll need it, but on the other hand, I don't really need their blessing do I? It's my life and no one in my family is that religious anyway."

"Traditions run deep and hard even if they are irrational."

"Ha! That's exactly what I would call all religions. Irrational beliefs. Jasmine shares my view on that subject at least, but she would like to think that I wasn't losing anything by being with her."

"Wise thoughts, I would say."

Having been there before, Raheem found the university grounds were a lot easier to navigate than the previous time. After parking the car, the two friends strode confidently towards the bookstore and their futures.

There were three queues of students eagerly waiting their turn at purchasing their curriculum material. In the case of Raheem and Reuben, they carried an email from their deans that simply stated that they could receive whatever was required for their courses and that no money need change hands. The quantity of the material was an unknown factor and quite surprised them both. There seemed to be an enormous amount of books, writing pads and laptops being amassed by the over-worked staff.

"I presume you will be wanting it all?" one of the staff asked Reuben.

"I guess so. Try not to mix his up with mine if you can."

"No problem there. Your boxes will have a big M for medical on it and his will have a big L for law. We've been doing this for quite a few years so you don't have to worry."

Raheem brought his car nearer to the doorway of the dispatch area, where the four boxes, each with their promised large letter, were waiting. The sight of each box cemented Reuben's feeling of exhilaration that he was finally on track to complete his medical course. His role in having helped his new friend also contributed to his feeling of satisfaction.

"Put your boxes in the back seat Reuben and I'll put mine in the trunk."

"Good idea."

Reuben was always impressed with the way Raheem had of coming up with sensible and logical solutions to things. *He was going to make a fine lawyer*, thought Reuben.

"Coffee?" asked Reuben.

"No thanks Reuben. I really need to start in on all of this. My first lecture is on Tuesday you know."

"Same here. I might need to get that licence and start driving pretty soon."

"It's my honour and duty to drive you, even if our classes don't quite match up, for this first year, if that's alright with you?"

"Sure it's alright. Let's see what workloads we have too. Tuesday morning then?"

"Eight-thirty I'm afraid. No walking with Jasmine to work anymore," he grinned.

"She'll understand."

Raheem drove away and Reuben placed the two boxes in the elevator and got them inside his apartment safely. The university staff knew how to pack things tightly, making sure that nothing would be damaged in the process. There was a list of all the items and Reuben decided to lay everything out on the floor and tick each one off. It took an hour to do it but it was worth doing. All the items were there and, looking at the floor, Reuben realized that a system needed to be implemented quickly, so he started taking items from the old lady's bookshelf and replacing them, methodically, with his medical books. He plugged in the laptop and started to charge its battery and then hung the new stethoscope over a chair. After taking the empty boxes downstairs to the big recycle bins, Reuben relaxed, made himself a coffee from the machine and just sat and stared at the books for quite a time.

At five o'clock, Reuben helped Jasmine lock up and they walked back to her place where she had a quick shower and changed into a simple yet elegant outfit. A dark blue skirt and a grey silk blouse. She looked delicious to Reuben, who was decidedly nervous about the dinner with his parents.

"They are going to love you as much as I do," he said when she emerged from her bedroom.

"I hope I like them," she laughed.

"At least you don't have to live with them. I've done it and it is not on the recommended list of things. However, my mother is a very good cook, you'll see."

As Reuben guided Jasmine through the streets, he couldn't help but think that the last time he had done this was with Hannah. Banishing that thought from his mind, he peered out the car window at the smoke coming from the chimneys of the houses they passed. This time, he did not feel any pang of jealousy at all. He was with Jasmine and there was no place he would rather be. Jasmine drove extremely carefully and pulled up outside the house with the porch light on. They looked at each other in anticipation and made their way to the front door. Jasmine knew that Reuben was well aware of everything she was feeling. There was no need for words.

Reuben let himself in and Jasmine breathed in the aromas of the Jewish cooking that wafted from the kitchen.

"Smells like my mother's cooking," she whispered.

"Hi Mum, we're here!"

As they walked past the hall of memories, Jasmine looked at the photos on the wall. She especially wanted to see ones of Reuben as a young child. There was one of Reuben's dad in full uniform that caught her attention. She was almost certain that the background was of her Lebanon, but she said nothing.

"In here Reuben," called back Sara.

Jacob was heavily involved in his newspaper, as was his ritual on most nights. Jasmine stared at him for a second trying to get a picture of this man who had been a soldier in her country, even if it was well before she was born. Jacob knew they were here and casually looked up. He was surprised, again, to see such a lovely girl with his son.

"Dad, I'd like you to meet Jasmine."

"Pleased to meet you Jasmine. Welcome to our home."

"Thank you sir. I'm pleased to be here too."

"Middle East I would say. Probably Lebanese? Am I right?" He asked the direct questions matter-of-factly.

"Yes sir, from Beirut."

"I was there a long time ago you know?"

"Yes, Reuben mentioned it and I saw your photo on the wall."

"Mmm. Can't say it was an enjoyable experience. Scared to bits the whole time I was there and couldn't wait to get back home."

Sara walked into the room and instantly laid eyes on Jasmine. So different to Hannah.

"Mum, this is Jasmine."

"Pleased to meet you dear," she said extending her hand.

"Me too Mrs. Cohn," said Jasmine shaking her hand.

"Just call me Sara if you like."

"Ok."

The usual Friday night ceremonies commenced and again Reuben did his best to explain them to Jasmine. Jasmine just watched as the blessings over the wine and bread were completed and they all had shared a small portion from the communal plate. Sara brought in a big bowl of chicken soup and ladled a decent scoop into the smaller bowls.

"Enjoy."

The soup was scaldingly hot and Jasmine had to blow on her spoon before she tasted it. Sara watched as she sipped.

"Do you like?"

"Oh yes, very much. Similar to what my mother used to make but she used a lot of lemon and sumac. Quite delicious."

"Thank you. I could give you the recipe if you like?"

"Yes please, I would like that. Thanks."

Roast brisket, potatoes and a green salad were served. Sara watched and waited for Reuben to pounce on them. She also had an eye on Jasmine and was pleasantly surprised to see her really enjoying the food. Reuben, however, was not doing his usual fast-eating act. Sara, surprised, started to feel a little worried about him.

"Are you ok Reuben?"

"Yes Mum, why do you ask?"

"Don't you like the food anymore?"

"I love your cooking," said Reuben smiling over at Jasmine.

"Reuben's made a few changes for the better. I told him that I wouldn't go out with him if he didn't," joked Jasmine.

"About bloody time too," blurted out Jacob and then resumed his eating.

"I never thought that part of him would ever change," said Sara, smiling at Jasmine. "I can only thank you, my dear."

"My pleasure. Anytime."

By the time the main courses were nearly finished, Reuben made a tinkling sound on his wine glass to get their attention.

"A couple of new things have occurred in my life of late. The most important is Jasmine and I have asked her to marry me. She is waiting a bit longer before she commits to it. The other is that I have recommenced my medical studies at C.U. and am in the process of buying an apartment not far from where I work at The Cook County Morgue."

There were a few moments of stunned silence, before Sara broke in.

"That's wonderful! Night school dear?"

"No Mum. I've actually swung a deal with The DA's Department so that I can study full time and still do the odd job or two for them while I complete the course."

Sara beamed proudly across the table.

"You are a bit of a dark horse aren't you?" chimed in Jacob. "I have news too. VA has given me a job securing advertising into their *Stars and Stripes* magazine."

Reuben feigned surprise. "That's great Dad. How's it going?"

"Slowly, I must say. Sold my first advert yesterday and today sold another two. So it's getting better."

"Mazeltov!" said Reuben and whispered to Jasmine, "That's congratulations in Yiddish."

"I thought it might be," she responded. "I've heard it before."

After Reuben had delivered all his monumental news, and the obligatory remarks made, his parents were a little quieter than normal. Possibly it was too much to absorb.

The meal was suitably rounded off with an apple compote followed by coffee and cookies. Reuben and Jasmine took leave of Sara and Jacob. As Reuben hugged his mother, he was surprised to glean that she was both extremely happy and proud of her son, but also a little amazed, as she had never had great expectations for him.

"See Mum, I guess you never thought I'd get to this point in life," said Reuben with a cheeky smile.

On the ride back home, it was clear that Jasmine had enjoyed the experience, even though it had brought back memories of her former family life that caused her some pain. Reuben had already picked up on it.

"This is our time now. We can't change the past, and we certainly can't live there either. It was what it was, and now we are going to forge out our own future."

"I liked your parents," she said with a smile.

"I think you miss a family around you."

"That too. They were not quite what I had expected though."

"Just people, like everyone else. My dad seems a bit mellower since his new employment. I'm glad you didn't see him a few weeks back, he was a real pain."

"No one's perfect."

Reuben was thrilled that the apartment came with an underground parking area. As he directed Jasmine into the bay reserved for him, the thought crossed his mind that maybe, when he got his driving licence, they could share a car. There was little need for two cars as Jasmine hardly drove hers at all.

The morning dawned crisp and clear. Although still chilly, the rain had stopped and Reuben could almost hope that better weather was finally coming. It seemed almost suitably prophetic for new beginnings.

Returning home from walking Jasmine to work, Reuben continued his revision of what he had completed in year one. Before he got started, he took a couple of steaks from the freezer and let them thaw out slowly on the sink. There were plenty of salad ingredients in the fridge so the night's meal was virtually planned.

His memory of medical school was quite sharp and by the time the evening came around he felt confident that going into second year would not be too difficult for him.

Reuben set the dining room table up very nicely with the plates and silverware neatly positioned. He'd picked a few flowers from a garden in the street and had placed them in a small vase that he'd found in the old lady's collection of assorted things. When he and Jasmine walked in from her work, she noticed them straight away.

"How sweet, Reuben. I love them, and I love you too."

"I love you too," he said giving her another kiss on the lips.

"What's for dinner?"

"Grilled steak and salad. I hope you'll like it."

"I'm sure I will."

Alberto Domenicci's American passport had been taken from him, and even though he possessed an Italian one, there were no possibilities to use it now. Travis Coffee had been summoned to do most of the legal work that kept Domenicci from being instantly put into remand. Coffee had argued to the court that it was only a coincidence that Domenicci had attempted to fly to Mexico on the day of the raid. There was no point denying the discovery of the drugs, but the strategy from here on was to delay the trial date as much as possible.

Domenicci was convinced that Hannah Martin had conspired with the FBI to rat him out, and that somehow Reuben Cohn from the DA's office was involved in it. He had been determined to make them all pay for it. Hannah was already dead and that left Reuben Cohn as a primary target to eliminate.

"Find out all you can on Reuben Cohn," ordered Domenicci to Travis Coffee.

"Who is he? How can it possibly help your situation now?"

"He's a District Attorney operative and I have to know what he knows."

"I'll check it out but I don't get it. This is an FBI matter."

"I know. Just do it."

"Alright."

Reuben and Jasmine went for a morning walk to check out the neighborhood. It was Sunday morning, peaceful and quiet. There were parked cars everywhere but nothing looked out of the ordinary.

In one of the cars a man sat reading his newspaper. He was in fact an FBI operative, on duty, keeping an eye on Reuben. He texted in, *Cohn walking with his girlfriend. All quiet here.* The man made an entry into his notepad and stayed in his car.

Reuben's new area was not so far from where they had each previously lived. But is was very apparent that this was far more upmarket than the shabby, industrialised zone in the vicinity of the morgue.

The circuit of the block only took twenty minutes. The FBI man texted, *Cohn and girlfriend back safely*.

As they were about to enter the elevator, Rose emerged.

"Hi neighbors," she said casually.

"Hi Rose," responded Reuben and Jasmine almost together.

"A drink at our place this afternoon around three work for you both?"

Reuben glanced questioningly at Jasmine. She seemed to like the idea.

"That would be lovely," she said. "Do you want us to bring anything?"

"Not really, very casual. See you then."

"Ok."

Rose sauntered off down the street as Reuben and Jasmine went up to the apartment.

Reuben texted Steve. *Hi Boss, having a drink with Travis Coffee this afternoon at 3, Reuben.*

Fast work. See what you can find out. Chat later.

Despite Rose's protestation that they should not bring anything, Reuben selected one of the more mature reds in the old lady's collection of wine. She had stocked up on a plentiful selection of fine wines, all of them in a price range much higher than Reuben would ever consider. Reuben's most expensive wine usually came to around eight dollars, including the tax. These wines must surely be in the forty plus dollar bracket, Reuben calculated. He figured that, even if he did not appreciate the difference in quality, Travis Coffee sure would.

Up one flight of stairs there was only a choice of two doors. Modern jazz could be heard drifting out from one of them so, without too much hesitation, Reuben knocked and they waited. After a few seconds he knocked again, more forcibly this time, figuring that the music probably filtered out the last attempt. The door opened and Travis greeted them jovially.

"Hi guys, I do like punctuality, come on in."

"So do I," said Reuben, handing Travis the bottle, and noticing the approving look.

"You really didn't need to, but it looks like a good one!"

The front door led straight in to a generous living area, in an apartment that was obviously much larger than Reuben's. Floor to ceiling glass commanded a stunning view of the surrounding streets. Modern furniture adorned the room and the softness of the cream-coloured carpet smacked of money – no expense spared. From here, one could see into the kitchen area with its huge bench space and trendy bar stools with leather seats and chrome legs. It was enough to impress anyone.

Rose and Shirley were seated at an elegant dining room table, engrossed in something on an Ipad. Rose closed the tablet, and they got up to greet the visitors.

"Oh my, what a pretty dress," said Rose looking admiringly at Jasmine.

"Thank you Rose. A lovely apartment," said Jasmine looking out their window into the street below. "Wow! Remarkable what an extra level can do for the view. Amazing."

"Yes it is a perk that we enjoy."

"Perk?" questioned Jasmine.

"Travis has a client who is extra keen to keep him happy and satisfied. He owns it and we live rent free here. He even did a special renovation to divide the apartment so that Travis's mother could live independently with us. We are one big happy family, aren't we Shirley, " Rose said nodding affectionately at her mother-in-law.

"You are lucky."

Travis uncorked the bottle and poured them each a wine. The elegant Kosta Boda glasses showed off the rich ruby colour.

"Cheers guys," said Travis as they clinked glasses. "Welcome to the neighborhood. Please, help yourselves," he said pointing to a carefully prepared platter of French cheeses, dried fruit, and nuts that was on the table. "By the way, what is it you do Nathan?"

"It's Reuben actually. About to start second year Medicine at C.U."

"Sorry, Reuben. Ah, C.U, my old college."

"I know," said Reuben casually, but enough to put Travis on his guard.

"Do you work?" he asked Jasmine, a little unsure of her name.

"Jasmine."

"Yep, sorry again. A lot on my mind of late."

"I'm the office manager of a driving school."

"Wonderful. You already know I'm a lawyer then, do you?" he said looking over at his wife.

"Oh yes," said Reuben, deliberately brushing past Travis to help himself to a piece of D'Affinois. "Your job can be quite dangerous, so I'm told."

There was a sudden uncomfortable silence in the room.

"What do you mean by that, Reuben?" asked a concerned Rose.

Reuben drew a deep breath and launched in. "There's no easy way to put this I'm afraid. I believe Travis has put your life and Shirley's at some risk. As well as his own."

"What sort of a joke is that?" Travis blurted out angrily.

"No joke. You know that you could face some serious prison time if convicted as a willing accessory to a murder? Of course you do. This client of yours has probably asked you to look into various people for him and I'm guessing that I'm on that list too."

"Are *you* Reuben Cohn?" Travis asked incredulously.

"I am. The FBI think that you are quite an innocent party at the moment. That will change once you tell your client that you've found me."

"How on earth do you know all of this?"

"Domenicci has tried to kill me once before and is itching to get it right this time. Unfortunately for you, he doesn't completely trust you either. He can't afford to trust people in the line of work he's in. You and your family are on his hit list as well. He is covering all the loopholes and you might have discussed something with your family that he didn't want talked about"

The silence was deafening as all eyes were on Travis.

Reuben pressed on. "Even if you didn't discuss any work issues at home, he is not going to believe you. Especially now that we are talking and drinking together. I'd say you are in the same boat as me, only I'm also a DA operative and you are swimming upstream against the big boys."

"I'm assuming that you are telling Travis this because you have a solution to this dilemma," said Rose coldly and quietly.

"I do have a solution. You may not like it, but it's the best I can think of at the moment."

"And that is?" asked Travis nervously.

"Downtown with me and we speak to the FBI guys on the case and you write a full report on Alberto Domenicci, and of course have no further dealings with him. We will know if you do. We knew this much didn't we?"

Travis's mobile phone buzzed. He looked at it and with some alarm saw that it was a text from Domenicci.

Travis, I'm downstairs about to come up, Alberto.

"It's him! He's coming up. What should I do?"

"Nothing. Act naturally and introduce me as Nathan Connors, your new neighbor. He doesn't know what Reuben Cohn looks like."

Travis stared agonizingly at Rose and his mother. Reuben texted Steve.

Boss, Domenicci coming up to Apartment 1 to see Coffee. Might need some assistance.

Steve's response was instantaneous.

I'll let the boys know just in case. Can't see him doing anything with so many witnesses around. Be cool.

Thanks Boss, will do.

A loud knock at the door, the sound of a key being inserted and the door opened.

"Travis?"

Willing himself to be calm, Travis mustered his bravado. "Alberto, what a surprise. Come join us for a drink. New neighbors, Nathan and Jasmine," said Travis as Domenicci made his way into the room.

Alberto Domenicci was a small man of around five foot five, wavy jet black hair, an Armani suit that would have been personally tailored for him and shiny tan crocodile skin shoes.

"So you bought the old lady's place. Beat me to it," Domenicci beamed as he shook hands with Reuben.

"Just lucky I guess."

With a calculated look, Domenicci eyed off everyone in the room then motioned to Travis to come and join him in the kitchen area.

"Just a quick word with your man, Rose."

"Sure, no problem," Rose said with a fake smile.

"Travis, I got a tipoff that the FBI were staking this place and I saw their car parked a little way away. Do you know anything about it?"

"News to me," Travis responded cautiously, hoping Domenicci couldn't hear the thumping of his heart and the tension in his voice. "What on earth for?"

"I don't know but I'm working on it. Did you find that Reuben Cohn for me as yet?"

"No one's heard of him. What's his connection to the case?"

"He's the one who started this whole investigation."

"Really?" said Travis quite bewildered.

"No telephones from now on. Can't risk the Feds listening in. Come to my office tomorrow at nine. Go back to your drinks," said Domenicci with a sinister grin as he made for the door.

"Sure Alberto, tomorrow?"

Domenicci was gone in a flash. Reuben watched from the window as he got into his Mercedes and drove away. Reuben texted Steve

It's ok, he's gone now. Not sure what he wanted. Reuben.

See if you can find out, Steve responded.

"What did he want?" asked Rose, obviously now having lost all semblance of calm.

"The FBI are staking out our place here and Alberto's getting a bit agitated," Travis informed her.

"The FBI?"

"That's probably for me, Travis," Reuben chimed in. "Nothing to do with you at all. But if Domenicci thinks that you are somehow cooperating with us, then my guess will be that he will have you taken care of quick smart. As well as Rose and your mum," said Reuben patting Travis on the shoulder. "He probably wants a meeting with you at his place tomorrow. Am I right?"

"How could you possibly know that?"

"Too many witnesses here," Reuben ventured.

"He only just this minute asked me for a meeting."

"If he's smart, and I'm guessing he is, then he will no doubt check up on who bought the old lady's apartment and when he sees my name there he'll know that you lied to him. What do you want me to do for you?"

"Shit! Shit! Shit! I've done it now haven't I?"

"I'll get you some protection, but we'll have to act quickly," said Reuben turning to face a desperate-looking Rose. By this stage, Jasmine had placed herself next to Rose, and was holding her hand comfortingly.

"Just do what he says, darling," Rose pleaded. "You don't fuck around with a guy like Domenicci. He's a killer."

"Alright, alright! Let me think!"

Reuben rang Goodall straight away and put his cell on loud speaker purposely so that everyone could hear the conversation.

"Boss, what can we do for Travis and his family?"

"He's prepared to write a full report?"

"He is shit scared and so am I for that matter."

"Sit tight. I'll get the FBI guy outside to take over and make sure there is backup here at the morgue as well. Don't move from the apartment, ok?"

"Got you. Thanks Boss."

"Wait a minute!" called out Travis. "Don't do anything just yet. I'll talk with Domenicci and resign."

"Tell him he's walking barefoot on cut glass," said Goodall over the phone.

"My life. My call!" yelled back Travis.

"Ok, call me if you need me, Reuben," said Steve, his usual reassuring self.

"Will do. Thanks Boss."

"What are you thinking? You can't reason with a man like Domenicci!" screamed Rose.

"I know what I'm doing," Travis assured her.

Reuben edged closer to Travis and patted him on the shoulder. Reuben immediately realized what was in Travis's mind. The lawyer was plotting to kill Domenicci.

"That's not a good idea, you know?" said Reuben quietly so that no one else could hear him.

"I'll talk to him first," Travis responded, looking utterly perplexed.

"No, I don't think so Travis. I hate him too, but don't even think about what you're planning."

"I can't live with this hanging over my family."

"The FBI will handle it."

"Sure!"

Travis grabbed his coat and bolted out of the apartment. Down the elevator, into the basement and into his car. Reuben watched him drive away while the three women stood there paralyzed and silent as if there was nothing they could say or do. Reuben texted Goodall.

Boss, I think he's going to try and kill Domenicci. What should I do?

Nothing at the moment. No law has been broken and he still works for the man. Let's see what he gets up to. Sit tight, I'd say.

Alright Boss.

Goodall telephoned the FBI and told them as much as he could about the conversation.

Travis sped across town in his navy blue Porsche Boxster. As per normal, he parked out front of the mansion of Albert Domenicci. Three stories of white marble with a garden and fountain right in front of the house. Very impressive, if you like that Italian Baroque style.

From the glove box of his car, Travis retrieved a small handgun. He checked that the cylinders were full and then put the loaded gun in his pocket. He'd never known this level of fear, anxiety and anger in his life. It was as if something had snapped inside him, triggered by the potential threat to his beloved wife and mother. His eyes burned with an unaccustomed fierce focus, and he felt a sheen of perspiration sticking his shirt to his back. He knew what he was going to do. Without locking his car, he strode purposefully to the front door and rang the bell. Albert looked through the peephole, and seeing it was Travis, opened the door.

"Did you find that guy yet?" Domenicci asked abruptly.

"Oh yes I did that alright," said Travis.

With a glazed look in his eyes, Travis put any other thoughts aside and focused on what he had come to do. Pulling out the gun, he emptied all six bullets into the head and chest of Domenicci, who barely had a moment to register his surprise before he dropped like a stone, dead, with blood pulsing all over the white marble doorstep. Hearing the noise, a maid scuttled to the doorway but Travis had already bolted back to his car. She watched in horror as he drove off with a screeching of tyres.

Travis knew he had crossed a line, morally and legally, from which there was no return. He'd saved his beloved family, but he knew there would be no saving himself, as the law would hand him a minimum of twenty-five years in prison. He knew he couldn't face that.

Travis was rapidly approaching the exit to the Monroe Street Bridge. A myriad of thoughts ran through his head, one of the stranger ones being how many years of pleasure he had got from his beloved sports car. Slamming the Porsche into third gear, he wrenched the steering wheel dramatically, driving the vehicle straight through the small retaining barrier, and plunging it fifty feet into the shallow river bed below. His beautiful vehicle, with the fancy trimmings, exploded on impact, but Travis was no longer alive to worry about it. It wasn't long before police cars, with sirens wailing, converged on the scene of Travis's demise.

Two FBI cars arrived at the Domenicci mansion. After calming the hysterical maid, and extracting a garbled summary of the events, one of the agents phoned through a report to Steve Goodall.

Goodall phoned Reuben immediately.

"Reuben, are you still at the Coffees?"

"No Boss. We are back in our apartment. Did he do it? Did Travis kill Domenicci?"

"He sure did. Hold on a minute – something coming through on the police info line . . . well, well! It looks like

Coffee has just driven his car off The Monroe Street Bridge. Reports are he's dead. The FBI will probably head up to your neck of the woods soon to inform his family. You will not be popular, I would think."

"I wanted to protect him!"

"They won't see it like that you know."

"I don't like this business, Boss."

For the first time since he had worked with Goodall on all these assignments, Reuben began to feel a deep sadness at the tragic outcomes of much of this style of work. At first he'd felt a sense of grim satisfaction and excitement, but now that feeling had changed. Sure, he'd helped to keep Jasmine, Steve and Travis Coffee's family safe, but the body count was now far too high. He felt a sense of relief that he was going back to the relatively safe environment of medicine.

Sesnsing the vulnerability in Reuben's voice, Goodall gave some worldy advice.

"Not your fault, but if you lie down with jackals you can't expect a good outcome, if you get my drift."

"I know," said Reuben resignedly.

"Speak to you later," said Steve and clicked off the line.

Reuben cuddled up to Jasmine on their sofa. She had an inkling of what had just been said and was smart enough not to mention it. She knew that Reuben would discuss it more fully with her once he decided the time was appropriate.

Unexpectedly he turned to her and asked, "Would you like a game of chess?"

"Sorry, I don't play that game," she replied." I do play backgammon, though. There's a set in one of the boxes I brought over."

"Let's play then," said Reuben, anticipating how different it would be to play a game with a live opponent rather than one hidden behind an online gaming identity.

Monday morning and the old routine kicked in for the last time. He accompanied Jasmine on her walk to work. Holding her hand, he became aware of something different. Fewer images of her thoughts filtered through to him. *Could be a good thing*, he thought.

Knowing that the following day the study routine would commence, he felt an odd pang of nostalgia for his old office. Swinging by the morgue, he headed up to his familiar work space, settled into his chair, and reassured himself that everything had been left on the desk in an orderly fashion.

He opened the refrigerated cabinet to find it completely empty. How long, he wondered, before he was called in to do another analysis of a found body part. He knew a part of him was going to miss the regular thrill of discovery that he was accustomed to.

For the rest of the day Reuben spent his time at home in a mixture of preparation and avoidance. First he organized his new backpack so that his study materials fitted in nicely. He also spent a couple of hours doing more revision on his past notes.

Paramount in his thoughts was to avoid the Coffees and the accompanying feelings of guilt over his part in what had happened with Travis.

Raheem had sent a friendly SMS reminder.

8:30 tomorrow Reuben, can't wait. How about you?

You bet. See you then, Reuben texted back.

Being on his own during the day, Reuben had a lot of time for reflection. All the incidents of the past few months had led him in a straight trajectory to where he knew, in his heart of hearts, he was always meant to be. His strange powers, even if they were perhaps diminishing, had both harmed and helped a lot of people. But foremost was his gratitude for having met Jasmine, and for the strengthening new friendships in his life. He'd never imagined himself as a person with close friends, but now Steve and Raheem could be counted in that category.

Reuben loved and respected his boss, but he knew that Steve was human. Confronting Jo with his infidelity would be one hell of a task. All Reuben could do, he decided, was to be as consistent a friend and workmate as possible, without any judgment attached to it. Raheem had called him brother. Reuben was starting to feel that way about him too.

Henry's it was for dinner. Jasmine specially selected the same booth where Reuben had saved her life, as she loved to put it.

"This will always be our seat. It's so exciting that you are going to become a doctor," she added proudly as they sat down.

"A few years to go yet," laughed Reuben.

"Your usual?" asked Henry as he poured the coffees.

"Not tonight Henry," said Reuben smiling broadly. "I reckon I'm going to have a shot at those ribs of yours. They look delicious."

"Good choice. What about you, young lady?"

"I'll try the pasta arrabiata," said Jasmine.

"Good choices!" Henry was proud of all the dishes on his menu.

At seven in the morning, Reuben's phone alarm buzzed annoyingly. He let Jasmine sleep a little more as he slid out of bed into the shower. She woke at the sound of the water and joined him under the hot water with a tender embrace and kiss.

Reuben made their coffees and toast and they sat in contented silence while they breakfasted.

By twenty past eight, Reuben had farewelled Jasmine and was already waiting outside the apartment when Raheem pulled up. Seeing Raheem's beaming smile, Reuben suddenly felt overwhelmingly moved.

"Good weekend?" asked Raheem

"It had its moments."

"It's really happening!" exclaimed Raheem.

"You betya it is."

THE END

www.ingramcontent.com/pod-product-compliance
Lightning Source LLC
Chambersburg PA
CBHW050307010526
44107CB00055B/2132